From

CHAINS

to

SAVED

ONE MAN'S JOURNEY THROUGH
THE SPIRITUAL REALM OF ADDICTION

ADAM VIBE GUNTON

To Aaron, Brendan and Chris
For stewarding God's message when I needed it most.

To My Family
For never giving up on me.

To My Nephew and Godson, Colton
For inspiring me to be an example.

To God
For sending Your Son to save me from the darkness.

TABLE OF CONTENTS

TO DUST WE
SHALL RETURN

I SAT NEXT TO MY attorney in a silent courtroom, preparing for the district attorney to present her pretrial evidence. I was inflated with a certain confidence that the evidence in this case would be suppressed from an illegal search and seizure. She walked over to the large television screen fifteen feet in front of me as my attorney leaned in close and whispered, "Are you ready?"

"Yep," I replied.

"Your Honor, the State presents Exhibit B from evidence for the court."

She pushed play on the DVD player and made eye contact with me as she turned to walk back over to her seat. White noise of a radio call came into the room. Staticky picture turns clearly to a vest cam on a police uniform walking briskly toward a police cruiser. A hand moves from the uniform, up past the camera. "What information do we have?"

He steps in his cruiser as dispatch responds, "Adult white male is reported to be asleep behind the wheel of a car at the stop sign at 1st Avenue and 1st Street. A movie has just let out, and patrons found the car running."

The cruiser's engine begins to roar less than half a mile down the road to find a 2016 Silver Chevy Cruze parked at a stop sign. He slowly creeps up to the bumper, blocking it from moving forward, and the first glimpse of me comes into frame—slumped over myself and not moving.

The cruiser door opens, and the radio sound is muffled out by the blaring rock music emitting from my car. The officer walks over to the driver-side door to find me lifeless, slumped over my seatbelt, with both eyes open. He reaches for the door handle; locked. His hand is now gripping his flashlight as he taps on the window. No response.

"HELLO?" he yells as he shines the light from his hand in my eyes. The music is blaring so loud from inside the car that he has to turn away to talk into his radio. "Driver is unresponsive and the door is locked. Can we get emergency medical here?" He turns back to the car, grips the roof with both hands, and shakes the car. My body slumps over to the right with no life sign.

Backup arrives. "Hey, park behind him. I'm going to break the window." The sound of the cruiser engine from a police cam is the exact vibrating roar it always was on COPS.

WHACK—the flashlight hits the rear driver's-side window. WHACK—again. CRASH—as glass shatters inside the back seat with the third swing and falls to the asphalt next to the car. He reaches in the window and unlocks the front door. The sound of the music is overpowering, and as he opens the door and leans in over me to put the car in park, I get the first glimpse of what my body looks like—dead—without a spirit inside of it. The vest cam does a close-up shot of my pale-skinned, open-jawed, wide-eyed, and lifeless body.

*The feeling of seeing your own dead body
on a 52-inch television screen in front of your face is
enough to take all the confidence of a won case out of
your chest. All you thought of your life, the meaning of
it, the invincibility of youth, and pride in who you
are is deflated from you in one breath.*

Thump thump thump as the car goes into park. The officer checks my pulse. "I can't find a pulse on him . . ." His hand moves from my neck to my nose. "He's not breathing. Check on medical and get them here STAT." His fist drives into my chest with its knuckles and shakes around on the sternum. This maneuver is intended to cause enough pain for the victim to wake up. It didn't work. "I'm going to get him out of here."

His hand reaches over and unbuckles the seatbelt holding me up, and he grabs my right shoulder to begin pulling me out. My left arm gets tangled in the seatbelt, and he pulls so hard I am released, slamming onto the asphalt with a loud thud, my feet still in the car. His arms reach up underneath mine as he pulls hard to release my legs before dragging me to the rear of the car, lying me in the pile of broken glass.

As he stands up, my arms are straight over my head, and my shirt had been pulled up to my neck, revealing my pale, breathless stomach riddled with skeleton-like structure. He stands up taller, moving the camera angle up past my body to my eyes—covered with a grey, smoky look. They were looking directly through the vest cam, through the television, and into my eyes—except not . . . They're not looking at anything. I'm not there. My eyes, without my spirit, stared straight into my soul in that courtroom, causing a feeling of being ninety years old, on my deathbed, without having accomplished anything. Regret. Guilt. Shame. Every form of condemnation flooded my mind and came out as wallowed-up tears and me choking to hold them back.

"Mike." I leaned into my attorney. "Can I leave?" I couldn't take another second of this torment.

"If you need to . . ." he said as he gave me a look that told me 'no.'

I took a deep breath and looked back up to the television screen.

Columbine High School

I REMEMBER TWO THINGS ABOUT fourth grade: we had super-cool salamanders in the classroom that I got to bring home for spring break, and the day the Columbine High School shooting happened. I was outside at recess at Columbine Hills Elementary when teachers began scrambling around and rounding us up with a kind of energy I had never experienced. They were confused, worried, and scared. So was I.

We were lined up like we normally were for the end of recess, but the teachers were loud with their commands and their bodies were tense. We were walked to and locked inside our classrooms. I remember the teachers would not, or could not, tell us what was going on. We were ushered to a corner of the classroom and the door was locked behind us. My teacher was behind her desk, crying, with a terrified look on her face and a radio attached to her ear. I was too young to try to listen to the radio for what was happening, so I was just reading her face and her emotions—they were passing on to me.

She kept us in that specific corner of the room, but I continued to leave that corner and go up to her desk, asking, "Ms. Maddox, are you ok? What's going on?" I was wanting to help her; I loved her.

"Go back over there." Her voice was terrifying, like all security and confidence had been drained from the spirit of my leader. I am getting chills and choking back tears as I write this to you from the still-present emotions of that day.

I don't know how much time had passed—maybe ten minutes—but I remember wanting to see my sister, who was down the hall in her sixth-grade classroom. I continued to disobey being put in a corner with my classmates because the feeling of fear was surrounding me and inside of me. I was trying to fly, which wasn't working, so I was doing what I could to fight back against being locked in this room. The classroom phone rang, and I had an overwhelming sense of relief when Ms. Maddox told me I was being called to meet my sister in the hallway to be picked up by my mother. My Mom was always there for us, like a Supermom. She was the first parent to pick up a student in my class. My relief quickly turned to even more confusion when she had to come to the front doors of our school to meet us and the principal. The principal unlocked the doors, let us out, and locked the doors behind us. As we got inside the car with my mom, she had me sit shotgun, an unusual command at this time of my life. During the five-minute drive home, she was crying and saying things I didn't understand. One that is grilled in my memory is, "They think they are gods!"

When we got home, my mother was glued to the TV screen and told me to stay in the house. She couldn't decide if she wanted me in the room with her watching the events unfold on the news just a few miles from where we sat. As the shooting was happening, brothers and sisters of classmates of mine were running from the school with their hands over their heads. I still have dreams from this. Sometimes in a crowded place—church, even—I can't help a daydream from coming into my mind of a shooter coming in, and what I would do when I saw him and caught him. These dreams started shortly after seeing these scenes on the news.

I lost one of my best friends whose older brother was killed. He just vanished off the face of the earth, and I never talked to him, heard from him, or knew where he went. I heard through the grapevine that his family couldn't handle it and left the community. Another childhood friend's neighbor used to bounce us super high on the trampoline because he was a cool older kid. He was killed. I didn't know what death was up to this point, and my first conclusion was death is when someone else takes your life with a gun.

When we were brought back to school after a break, a childhood counselor was brought through every classroom to offer someone to talk to. I remember his tall, big body standing next to my much smaller teacher at the front of the classroom when she said, "He has been brought in to talk with anyone who is struggling with the events that have been taking place. Raise your hand if you would like to talk with him."

My hand shot up before thinking. I looked around, as no one else's hand went up, and everyone else's head turned towards me. Mine immediately shot down, and I felt embarrassed as I was brought out of the classroom to speak with him. My young mind was so confused that I was only able to muster up, "I just don't get it. Why? Why would someone do that?"

He didn't have an answer for me. He seemed to be dealing with the same question rolling around in his own head. His big body sitting across from me at that little school table made me feel some sort of comfort in humor. I took that comfort with me wherever I could find it.

FAITH

IT WAS MY JUNIOR YEAR at Columbine High School. I was enjoying growing into knowledge of myself and my identity as a high school athlete on the football and wrestling team. The cool thing about being on a team at this point of my life was that I was never alone. We looked after each other in many ways. Although we didn't have the look-out-for-eachotherness enough to keep each other from drinking and partying, one of the ways we did so responsibly was by not allowing one another to drink and drive. We would not risk anything like that for ourselves and the team. The rule was: you either stayed at the house you were partying at, you did not drink, or you had another football player that was not drinking drive you home. This night, Ty (our six-foot-three-inch, two-hundred-eighty-five-pound, four-point-six-flat-forty-running senior D-end) was my driver.

The parents of a good friend whose house we were partying at left us kegs when they went up to Black Hawk to gamble for the night. There were six of us at the house early to set up the beer pong tables and different powwow seating arrangements for people to mingle comfortably. After we had finished setting up and tapping the kegs, I played a couple games of beer pong with two of the other guys (I won, of course) then sat down to the right of Ty on a neighboring chair. We were all laughing and having a good time, getting excited about the party to come.

I was in a conversation with Travis (our offensive tackle I had just beat at beer pong) from across the table. My Solo cup was just about empty, so I tipped it back and finished it off. As I began to stand up for a refill, Ty asked me, "Hey, we are staying here, right?"

"Heck yea!" I replied.

"Can I get a beer, then?"

"Sure!" I took the few steps over to the keg, and, while filling up my cup, I grabbed a second for Ty. I filled it up and went back to take my seat next to him. I turned to my left with a smile and handed him his cup. As I shifted my gaze back to Travis and began lifting that beer to my lips, something happened that I will never forget.

Some kind of energetic force entered into me at the top of my head and pulsed through my body all the way to my feet. My toes were tingling, my hands were weightless, and that plastic cup froze in midair. I was no longer in control of my body. Terror gripped my soul, and my mind was no longer my own. Ty had been lifting his beer on cue with mine, and just before he tipped it to his lips, my left hand shot over with force, stopping it in its tracks. Our heads turned to each other at the same moment, and my eyes looked directly into his with an intensity I had never experienced as I said, "Ty, we gotta go."

To this day, Ty says the reason his only response was a quick, "Okay," before we left was because he, "saw something else talking to him through me." We left right before anyone else showed up and went about our night alone together. We were in his car somewhere that night when we got the call about the shooting.

The owner of the house—we will call him 'James,' was my best friend at the time, and we are still friends to this day. At that time in my life, searching for identity, we were seen as the 'bad-asses' of the city when it came to fighting and rival high schools. Really, James was the biggest and baddest of them all, and I was just in his crew. I was always next to James.

After Ty and I left that night, a lot of people showed up and the party got going. This was interrupted when a gang showed up wanting in the party. Apparently, James' sister was dating one of the gang members not knowing he was in a gang. He brought all his friends dressed in their colors to come into the party. James was at the front door holding it open and telling them, "We can't let you in this party. This is a high school party, and we just don't want you here," and had another friend standing next to him at the open door, where I would have been standing.

After arguing for a little longer and throwing insults back and forth, James yelled at his sister, who was standing in the street to, "Get your ass in here!" right before three of the gang members pulled out guns and opened fire on the house. The friend who was standing next to James turned to run down the hall away from the shooting, and was hit in the back of the head and killed. Two other kids were injured.

CHUCK

MY EYES BEGAN TO FLUTTER open with a heaviness from the alcohol I had consumed the night before. My mind was trying to grasp where I was as I woke up to a small vibration shaking my knee and my ringtone blaring loudly from underneath unfamiliar sheets. I was still so drunk I could barely move. I vaguely remembered the girl whose bed I was in as she softly groaned and kicked her leg at my phone. I bent my body and lifted the white comforter to reveal light blue satin bedding with a small phone screen light shining from underneath it. The bed was so smooth, so comfortable in that moment as my hand glided between the softness to find my hardened phone.

I gripped it and blinked a few more times, getting used to the light coming off it as it continued to ring. The date and time read September 28, 2008, 4:47 a.m., and my best friend "Chucker" was calling me. A thought immediately came to my mind of a decision I needed to make in that moment: I could answer the phone as if it was any other time of the day, with enthusiasm to hear from him like, "Hey! What's up, Chuck?!" or I could answer the way I was feeling with, "Ugh. Hello?!" I chose the latter, to which a soft voice replied, "Hey, what's up?"

I continued my frustration with, "Dude, why are you calling me this late?!"

"I just wanted to call and say hi," he replied.

"I'm sleeping. Don't call me this late again." And I hung up, cuddling back up with the girl whose name I don't remember, and whom I never saw again.

The next morning, after I had had a few more hours of sleep, my friend Brian came to pick me up and take me back down to Denver to my aunt's house for a family party. I was enjoying the food put together for a big Italian family when my phone began to ring. The small screen read another close friend of mine's name, Trent. There was no decision to make. "Hey! Wassup, buddy buddy?" as I always answered the phone for him.

"Hey man." His tone was much softer spoken and unenthusiastic.

"I don't know how else to say it, so I'm just gonna say it. Chuck's dead, dawg."

My stomach dropped as my body went into a state of shock, and my insides began to boil with adrenaline. "What? What do you mean?" was all I could get out.

"Yea, dawg. Chuck shot himself last night."

I fell to the floor on the carpet next to my aunt's front door. Tears began to stream down my face, and I told Trent I would call him back.

For the next few days, I was surrounded by friends of mine and Chuck's. I was boxed up and locked away from the reality of what was going on. All my friends were consoling me, loving on me, and grieving with and for me as Chuck's "best friend." We were spending time together as a group at someone's house. I was closed off to all the affection as I laid on their couch for hours staring at the ceiling. Everyone was drinking, but I couldn't even comprehend how to stand up, let alone drink. The feeling of loneliness and emptiness was only magnified by the thought, 'I can't tell anyone about the phone call. This is my fault.' I had nothing to say for the first couple days, only empty hugging and head nodding. The pain was so immense and the sadness so deep that the feelings weren't manifesting. I was a blank body. Hollow.

There was an opportunity to go meet with a friend who was at the apartment where Chuck committed suicide the night it happened. He and I had a drug deal to make, and he had a story for me, so I mustered up the strength to push off the couch to go meet with him.

"Yeah, man, I saw it happen," he began. "We had just gotten back from Shotgun Willie's in Denver and were chillin' on the couch. He wanted to make a phone call—I think it was actually to you . . ." My bones ached as I listened to him continue. "Then, a minute later he growled and stomped through the living room past me to his bedroom. I heard him open his drawer, and then a click from him pulling the trigger. He pulled the trigger a second time, and it clicked. I jumped up off the couch and yelled, 'Chuck no!' as he pulled the trigger the third time and the gun went off. I was stepping into his room as his body fell to the floor."

This story solidified my belief that this was my fault. That friend, to my knowledge, did not share that phone call with anyone. And neither did I, for eight years, as I bottled it deeper and deeper down with drugs and alcohol. That drug deal we had to make? That was the first time I was introduced to OxyContin. That was also the first time I consciously used drugs to mask my feelings. No more partying just for fun, no more drugs are cool . . . No, drugs had now become my answer. Drugs were my solution to life.

WAKE UP

This is a story of broken hearts,
Hearts misrepresented through ideas brought on by misunderstanding.
Through the valley of death we have gone,
We stand strong, united in a song.

She was prematurely born to a mad mom.
The thoughts came early to this glad girl.
Dad kicked her out for a lesson 'bout this sad world.
Bad drug habit taught and shown but never alone.

Moved to the streets at fifteen, forced to be grown,
With a hat flipped back and a bill marked fresh,
Shirt, jeans, and shoes, with an empty backpack,
Laughed at, fun-poked, flicked behind the ear.

Trying her best just to make it through the school year,
Tears flowin' like the river she slept next to.
Her eyes to the sky, asking why nobody even cares.
Right then, she heard a Bic flick by the bridge.

With her own intentions and what her father made her witness,
She went to check if the guy with the blue durag and black eyes
Would show and tell if life is really all about
Getting high . . .

Addiction, I'm addicted to the struggle.
Addiction, I'm addicted to the trouble.
Addiction,
Not addicted to anything but searching for life and how to live it.

Too bad lessons in class never taught her what her gift is.
Classes with assholes looking for asses.
The teacher glared at her during her rare attendance.
Passing grades turned empty chair and her absence.

She left, never to return, looking to learn.
She ran with that man, double-age like her dad.
First week went smooth, high off weed and some booze.
She was searching for love everywhere but in and above.

Dreams of love awoken and broken by doves explodin'.
Her weak legs unexpected, with a tight grip on her neck, 'n'
Breath lessened with a pillow on her head then,
Her body stayed alive, but her soul stayed half past dead.

Her stolen innocence was attempted way before this.
Six years old when dad showed her what her chore is.
She pours soul out on paper, ink blotted with tears,
Dried only by her voice, rejoiced as she says,

Addiction, I'm addicted to the struggle.
Addiction, I'm addicted to the trouble.
Addiction,
Not addicted to anything but searching for life and how to live it.

Just an old soul trapped in a body of neglect,
Respect demanded by a man and his ego.
Evil shows uncontrolled from those shown a thrown,
By God locked in man's dungeons getting shock treatment.

Gifted a confused spirit lifted to the ceiling!
I battle I battle I battle, and I always lose.
Suffering and pain, I can't explain this is what I choose.
I'm an unlit fuse left by an 8-ball bomb.

I cruise the streets looking for maternal things.
I tell my one and only that I love her to her eyes,
And at night I sleep, wishing to die,
Never to wake up and never to remember memories!

So I gotta do what I gotta do.
I'd check this mic but learned to talk at age grade 2.
I've got a story that I've got to get out.
Vibe's eyes cry as I scream into the sky!

Too bad he can't talk back when I'm yelling, can you hear me?!
I was fourth born, thrown to the floor,
Scarred legs to this day from my diaper worn fourscore.

Momma fed her baby cocaine-laced milk meals.
Momma never hugged me to show me love was real,
So Momma never bothered teaching me not to rob and steal.

I was told to take a nap in the fourth grade,
So give me my hourly wages that are unpaid!
Money couldn't save me 'cuz I'm carrying a dollar to my name,
Shame from my heart for where my thoughts keep going,

Feelings darker than the eyes behind my blue mask,
Tasked with a mindset that everyone is evil!
Attracted padded rooms doomed to prove my point,
With coined eyes by Hades, I'm taking everybody with me.

Saved for a blink of an eye until I saw through,
Graduated high school, something adoptive siblings didn't do.
True to my heart, an empty mass in my chest,
But I guess, what could I expect when I'm just
An addict,
I'm not just an addict . . .

The screeching of the ambulance siren echoes through the courtroom as I lie there on that television screen, alone and desperate, with my eyes looking up to the sky as if I could see right past all the troubles this earth brings—leaving behind all the joys I was missing out on. The ambulance stops behind the camera that never turns to see it arrive. The backup officer fills in the paramedic as she sets down her bag of supplies next to me. She looks up at the camera and asks the officer behind it if I had shown any movement. The camera shakes slightly from side to side, and she turns her attention to me. As she begins to kneel towards me, my chest shoots up in the air and I sit up with life filled back into my eyes. A deep breath fills my lungs, and I become immediately aware of the situation I had just come back to life into—on that screen, and in my defendant seat. I was embarrassed and amazed. Grateful and changed. Alone and afraid.

The case was continued, but that case is not my story. I swore off heroin that day in the courtroom, because I saw the divine intervention that had happened on video. Seeing your lifeless body brought back from the dead is enough to wake anyone up to the reality of the spiritual realm of life. Or so I thought.

The Highway

THIS EXPERIENCE OF SEEING MYSELF on a T.V. screen being brought back to life woke me up to another experience in 2014, in the grips of my addiction, driving from Texas to New Mexico to pick up a much-needed load of dope. I was in Texas on what we called in the satellite sales industry a 'blitz,' where a group of salesmen would go to a town for a period of a week or two, stay in a hotel together, and sell every day for ten hours a day and make as much money as possible. At this one, I had planned out to bring two eight balls (seven grams) of heroin with me, and to use a half gram per day to make it through the two-week blitz. I was out on day four, and by day five was beginning to get sick. I don't remember the lame excuse I made to drive back to New Mexico, but I made one nonetheless, and started my two-day trek on day six. I was driving a company truck, withdrawing from opiates, eleven hours to my destination.

An addict in the throes of addiction is
willing to do anything for the fix they need;
what do we need to be willing to do to recover?

I was around halfway through the drive when I found myself on a winding mountain highway with a speed limit of 60 mph, with one lane of traffic in either direction. There was a beautiful drop-off mountain landscape with green tree hills as far as I could see to my right, while light tan rock mountains made up the wall to my left, past the lane of oncoming traffic. I had begun to come out of the fog of being actively high, and withdrawal had fully set in. The clarity of my vision and the colors of the scenery were something I wasn't used to at the time; neither was the feeling of drowsiness and body fatigue. I began thinking of my grandpa who had recently passed, and about my family, who I had been unable to be present with at the funeral without being high. The smell of the trees was peaceful, the vision of my family and talking with them was serene, and, all of the sudden, my withdrawal symptoms in my body had passed.

I enjoyed this feeling for what seemed like an eternity—walking around with my family and talking to my grandpa. I remember a smile coming on my face as I looked at him. Just before I made it in to hug him, I felt something punch me in the chest with such force my breath was knocked out of me with a sigh. My eyes opened to being in the wrong lane of traffic ten car lengths from a semi-truck coming around a bend, headed straight for me. The timing of me waking up was so immaculate that I merely turned the wheel slightly to the right to correct into my lane with one second left before the giant truck came barreling by with a deadly wind shaking my truck.

This gust of wind I felt from the semi was surpassed by a Presence I felt in my truck. I had a familiar tingling feeling in my limbs and head when a Peaceful, Comforting thought came into my heart. It wasn't audible, just Peaceful. A Presence of closeness with my Creator. I looked up at the sky through the ceiling of the truck, and lipped with wide eyes, "Thank You," just before another gust of wind left from my heart, swirling around the cab of my truck and out the windows. The onset of my withdrawal symptoms came back instantly.

ANGELS

I WAS NEARING THE END of my court process when I decided I wanted to go out to California, where all my belongings were in storage, to donate them. I wanted to start a whole new life with my past washed off. My mom flew up to Montana to meet me, and we drove my work truck out to California to take everything I had out of storage and donate it to the Veteran's Transition Center of America. For some reason throughout my life, sacrificing to help others has always made me feel better about myself. I have always genuinely wanted to make a difference in other people's lives. I also had a habitual pattern of building up a life around me and crashing it down to nothing, before taking what I did have left and giving it away so I would feel I was adding value to the world. My insane contribution.

On our way back from California to drop my mom off in Colorado, we made it to Las Vegas. We found a shabby hotel to stay the night at. I told my mom I was going to go gamble—you know, since we're here—but I was really going to find some dope. I did my normal creep around the city until I found a more run-down and rough-looking part of town. I stopped at a gas station, where I saw some familiar-looking crowds congregating. It was dark, and some of the lights of the 7-11 were out, which made it look even more ominous. I never really dealt with nerves when approaching strangers I knew had drugs. Door-to-door sales taught me how to get whatever I want, wherever I want, whenever I want. These were my people; I just had to show them I was cool. I walked up to a young woman who had just walked out of the 7-11 from the slot machine, and asked her, "Do you know where to pick up?" She was a well-known prostitute in the area, so right when she told me, "Yeah, do you have a car?" I was being watched.

We walked over to my truck and hopped in. During a brief conversation about what the plan was, and before I was able to put my keys in the ignition, I noticed a police officer a block-and-a-half away had pulled out of an alley behind the 7-11. He was waiting in the shadows for me to drive off to pull me over. I could see him in my side mirror from a streetlight spotlight coming perfectly down on his face, staring at us like we were a donut ready to be demolished.

I calmly said to her, "Don't look, but there is a cop behind us, getting ready to pull us over. I'm not going to start the truck."

Her heart began racing, and I could feel her fear and anxiety as she said, "I can't have another contact with them. Why are they messing with me? We ain't even doin' nothin'."

I intuitively knew what to do and replied, "It's okay. If he comes over here, just let me talk to him. We are going to slowly get out, leave my truck here, and walk where we need to go." I noticed as I got out of the truck with her and looked over at the police car that he knew his plans were foiled. We walked slowly together across the street from where I was parked and ducked into an alley. I looked back as the police car drove up and parked behind my truck to run the plates. I knew we were in the clear. She began thanking me, and was very relieved at the way we had just gotten out of the situation. We took a left down another alley, getting fully out of view of where we had come from.

We had made it about half-way down this dark alley when I began to say, "So, I want to get a gram of . . ." At that moment, in mid-sentence, I got a whiff of something foul and heard a small voice from a higher realm come through my head and land in my heart, saying, "Turn around . . ." In an instant, something came over my body like electricity coursing through my bones. My left arm was raising in a defensive straight blocking position, and, right when my eyes got turned around, a man was three to five steps behind me, with a doubled-up fist, looking straight at my head. He was coming at me at a fast pace to knock me out from behind!

My eyes drilled with fire into his eyes, as I said with a resounding deep tone, "Wrong guy!"

He saw something in me that scared him so badly his eyes almost popped out of his head as he tried to stop, only managing to fall in a puddle of water catching himself with his left elbow. He continued trying to get up and run away, but was falling over and over, tripping over his own feet as he was looking back at me with an energy I had never seen before.

I have seen terror portrayed in movies, but the way this man looked at me was of reverent fear. The electric charge in my bones flew out as quickly as it entered, and I watched him for a few more seconds before he turned the corner of the alley, out of sight. I was reflecting on the voice I had heard and the experience of the Spirit entering my bones, when I looked over to the woman helping me find drugs. Her hands were clasped in front of her chest, staring at me in amazement.

I have found in my life that no matter where I am or what I am doing, God never leaves me or forsakes me. This is one of many times, some you are reading in this book, that the voice of God or an instance with the Holy Spirit has saved me from a very bad situation. Of course, the woman and I continued our journey and I got my fix before returning to my truck unharmed.

God never loved me any more, or any less, than He does in this moment. He watches over me and protects me in all my ways. It is fun to look back at all the things He has done for me that I was asleep to at the time.

PAIN

I LOOKED DOWN AT THE syringe I had just prepared at my computer desk in my Glendale, Colorado, corporate housing apartment. I was on an interstate work leave from my Montana probation sentence, where I had made a promise to my probation officer to do everything right. My thoughts began a familiar series of questions:

'How am I here again? How did this happen? What am I doing? Is this life even worth it? I don't want to do this . . .'

I felt so empty, so hopeless, so lonely, so broken and powerless that I began to cry. My vision was blurry as I looked through the tears at the loaded solution. This solution that was no longer working. This solution I had come to rely on that was taking everything from me over and over in my life. I set it on my desk before my face fell into my hands as I cried out loud, losing my breath from the depth of the pain.

PRAY . . .

I heard a Voice, causing my eyes to come out of my palms and look behind me, above my right shoulder.

Nothing was there. My face went back into my hands with a deep moan, inducing more tears.

PRAY . . .

31

I heard it again clearly, and knew Who it was. My body was so weak from the battle I could barely get the strength to take the four steps over to the end of my bed, before falling to my knees to catch my breath.

"GOD . . ." was all I could get through my pain, and before I could think of what to say, I felt a pair of arms wrap me up from behind and embrace me with a hug. The Arms were not coming from a standing position, they were coming from someone kneeling on the floor with me. My breath was instantly restored, and a sense of calmness and Peace came over me. I laid my face onto the bed and didn't say another word. I rested in His arms for fifteen to twenty seconds and was completely released from the state I was in.

I stood up, walked over to my desk, and shot up.

These are all stories, full non-fiction.
Tales of wandering souls lost in addiction.
The past is all that's had when tomorrow ain't predicted.
Always-present sorrow, death is on the Christmas wish list . . .

It's a tough hand to play, growing up like no one loves you,
Mom trying to get you while you hide inside the bathroom.
Seven years old, and younger brother's minus two,
You're protecting him, hoping doors protect you.

Then a knife comes through, and you scream,
"Mom, I'll clean my room!"
And this is normal, or so you learn.
Karma burns, what did kids do to deserve this?

Broke away from literal chains, and they judge you cuz you're
homeless?
Different perspectives, like what a home is;
You bum cigs and lift spirits—isn't that what love is?

You trust all this, thirteen years after seven,
Till the call which reminded of your promise.
Old turns new when you learn you can't protect him,
Cuz demons got him, and now his life is spent in prison.

Miss him, wishin' to go with him, countin' ten friends need
protection,
In hotel rooms that you've rented, said you'd keep 'em warm and
meant it.

I want to take the pain away, I want to take the pain away,
I want to take the pain away, I want to take the pain away . . .

If I could take the pain away from all the addicts that are suffering
and put it on myself by spending eternity in Hell, I'd sign the contract
with both realms, go today, and say I'm happy with the hand that I
was dealt . . . but I can't.

You are beautiful—but no one tells you.
You look at men as projects meant to attend to.
Loss of innocence at two, lost connection to your value,
Mom let 'em shop her kids as child prostitutes.

Your bright heart shadowed for a hit of black tar,
Now your purpose is these searches for another lover.
Can't attract to 'em unless you can take away their suffer,
Give and can't receive, but take the blame from on your mother?

Cuz you love her, too.
Drugs cover it up so you can act like nothing bothers you.
Truth is, it all does.
Wondering 'bout life, if this wasn't what was.

So it must be, the fuel for your journey.
You're done with a man when his spirit's back to working.
Turning your back, an act of always learning,
Hoping no one notices your soul inside is really hurting.

I want to take the pain away, I want to take the pain away,
I want to take the pain away, I want to take the pain away . . .

If I could take the pain away from all the addicts that are suffering
and put it on myself by spending eternity in Hell, I'd sign the contract
with both realms, go today, and say I'm happy with the hand that I
was dealt . . . but I can't.

I write emotion-invokin' decoded stories to be spoken.
My regrets of the past die every time I cry on a line and face y'alls
judgment,
So judge it. There's only One.

You ever pressed on your temple with the barrel of a loaded gun?
Wondering why the trigger is immovable by your finger?
Lingering on the brink of death, your heart is pounding in your chest,
Thinking of the friends who've left, and wondering if they'll miss you.

Nah, cuz your vision of the funeral is a church full of empty pews.
I said I hate you, but I didn't mean it.
Then I said thank you, but I didn't mean it.

All of this pain paid for a point with some liquid?
I believe there is a cure for this current epidemic.
Red dots falling on the middle of my page,
Bleeding tears through my eyes 'til insights come out to say:

Christ can take the pain away. Christ can take the pain away.
Christ can take the pain away. Christ can take the pain away.

During this time, I began to build up a debilitating hatred for the perpetrators of these crimes on children—a hatred so deep that I began to devise plans on how I was going to be a child molester serial killer. When people would tell me the stories of their fathers, uncles, men in trusted positions for care, and all the other unprosecuted abusers, I would very methodically ask questions throughout the process that would find out where they lived. I thought I had found my life's purpose. I had watched *Dexter* about seven times, all the way from episode one to the last episode, so I would say I was an expert on how to get away with these plans I was devising.

Part of my plan included needing money. I had to make a large amount of money so I could support my drug habit as well as get tools and a good place to have my secret serial killer lair. I got a call about going out to South Carolina to continue selling DIRECTV in an AT&T U-verse area. So began my lone cross-country drive from Billings, Montana, to Columbia, South Carolina. I brought just enough dope to last me the drive, so I would run out as I got there and be able to work for a month or two while I planned my new life as a lurking masked man in the shadowy corners of the child molester's home; waiting to come out with the long icepick straight into their liver. The visions I had were deafening.

When I neared my destination's exit, I was having one of these visions of exactly what I was going to do with one of my victims. The torture I was going to put onto this man was going to be epic. My creative mind was now completely fixated on how to cause the most unimaginable pain possible to these people. I was driving on the highway with my cruise control set to seventy, my foot planted to bring my knee high enough to rest my elbow, and my thumb and pointer finger cupping my chin in deep thought like one of those Greek statues. My thoughts were plummeting from who I truly was in my heart. They were reaching such a deep hatred for a group of people that I felt the Holy Spirit leave my heart. Just then, I could feel the protection that surrounds me, that we are often unconscious to, fleeting. It was a space vacuum inside my truck. Fear suddenly gripped me in a way I hadn't experienced since my junior year of high school before that party. This time, though, I felt as though a hand had gone through my chest and was squeezing the life out of my heart.

I took my hand from my chin and gripped the steering wheel, attempting to squeeze it harder than what was on my heart. The harder I squeezed, the less I could breathe. My thoughts were racing about hatred for these criminals, but were now being confused by questions being asked from somewhere not of my own volition:

"Why do you want to kill these men?"

"They did horrible things."

"Yes. What will the outcome be if you kill them?"

Anger gripped me, and my chest tightened.

"He will be dead and punished for what he did!"

"Is it your place to be judge? Is it your place to be punisher?"

"They deserve it! I want them all dead!"

"There will always be another evil person."

"I know, but what am I supposed to do?"

"What is it you really want?"

I thought hard. I searched for why I really wanted to kill all these people.

"I want all my friends' pain to go away, and I want them to find You, and find freedom from all this hurt. What am I supposed to do?"

"You shall not repay evil with evil. Forgive and repay evil with love."

With this command clearly spoken to me, and the weight of a bodybuilder's grip strangling my heart, I took a deep breath and prayed aloud in my truck,

"Father God! Would you forgive these men? Forgive them for what they have done. Break the hold of generational abuse, Lord Jesus, and give them the same opportunity at salvation as I have been given. Lord God, I pray blessing over the victims of these crimes. I pray blessing over the abusers, to find You, God, to stop their evil ways and have the opportunity to come to You. Holy Spirit, I pray that You would help guide me away from hate and malice and toward love and forgiveness for all."

As I prayed this, I felt the stranglehold of hate on my heart release. A hand gripped so tight on my heart that I couldn't breathe correctly, and as I prayed earnestly for the forgiveness of the men I was planning on murdering, I felt the grip release in an instant, and I felt the Spirit re-enter into my heart. That all-too-familiar feeling of tingling throughout my body and the overwhelming Peace that comes along with it became present in the truck.

Ideas started to flow into my consciousness from somewhere beyond my own intellectual idea generation. I began seeing billboards with big bikers next to highways with slogans like, "We will protect you." I began seeing visions of an abused child, scared and alone in a car with her abuser, seeing this billboard and gaining hope of getting out of the situation. I saw this same little girl sitting in front of the television at home when a commercial came on of big burly bikers saying, "Are you a victim of abuse and looking for a way out but scared of what will happen? Call this number and talk to one of us about options you have. Your abuser will not know about you calling if you do not want them to. Please call. We are here to help you and protect you."

My visions began getting deeper and deeper about how many children there are out there going through the beginning stages of trauma that can be stopped before it is too late. I started envisioning faces of dozens of children around the country seeing these billboards and commercials. They were finding hope and a new life through private non-profit protection services that made them feel safe and gave them a new lease on life. I saw the process unfold and smiles on all their faces by the end of my vision. I heard the voice come back into my heart,

"You are not here to punish or hate. You are here to love and protect."

The sense of Peace overpowered all the plans I had been making for over a month, and all the killer mentality left me for good. And, wouldn't you know it, one of the main stewards of God's message to me at the end of my addiction was a convicted child molester. In no way do I condone or accept child abuse in any way. However, if this experience in my truck hadn't happened and I hadn't been able to hear the message from the messenger, I might not be writing this to you today.

Unseen to Seen

I ROLLED THE WINDOW DOWN slightly to feel the cool mountain breeze and smell the pine trees. She was giving me directions into a dark abyss of windy, one-way dirt roads with only enough room for my borrowed work truck to fit between the forest. Good thing I was in this truck, because my Camry wouldn't have made it.

After driving for ten minutes, we came to a clearing and found a trailer house that looked like it had been hand-built for the movie *The Hills Have Eyes*.

As we walked in the front door, the living room was to the right, and went straight back to sliding glass doors leading to a hand-built blacklight hot tub room. To the right, through the living room, was a door that went into the owner's bedroom. To the left was the kitchen; and through the kitchen went a walkway into a hallway to a bathroom/laundry room and a bedroom. It was the girl I was with, the owner of the house, and two other girls hanging out in his room smoking together.

After I had been through the house several times on trips from the back room, to the kitchen, to the other back room, and back again (meth does this to you), I sat down in the owner's room for a while with him and the three girls. I shared some of my music with them, like I always did when I had the opportunity, and people continued to take trips back and forth to the bathroom, the kitchen, or wherever else. This time, I finished a song and let them know I was running to the restroom really quick.

Again, I walked from his bedroom, straight through the middle of the living room, through the kitchen, and into the laundry room/bathroom. I finished up and came walking out through the kitchen. As I was stepping from the kitchen into the living room, my eyes became fixed on the center of the living room floor. Lying in the middle of the floor, as if placed there on purpose, was a Bible. Right when I recognized the Bible, the two girls who were with the owner walked out of the bedroom talking to each other. Before I could get out the words, "Watch out for the . . .," they had already taken a step perfectly over it without even breaking stride or conversation, as if it was somehow protected.

My eyes got wide as we moved past each other and I took steps towards the beautiful old Book lying on the ground. I hadn't seen it there the other ten trips I had taken through the house. I bent over and picked it up. It was old—like, really old. I opened it up, and it was in a translation I had never seen before. It was beautiful. I felt the Power coming off of this Book into my fingertips, and my jaw dropped as I flipped through the pages to the Red Letters. I examined it for a few more moments in awe before taking it back to the owner's room and asking him, "Whose Bible is this?"

"I don't know," he answered. "I've never seen it."

"What do you mean?" I insisted. "I just found it on the living room floor." His face got a little annoyed as I turned my shoulder to point to the floor where I had found it.

"Look man, I don't know whose ****ing Bible that is. I don't know anyone that would bring that in here."

At the time, I was standing in wonder because I just wanted to find the owner of the Bible and have a talk about where it had come from. I found all the girls and asked them. The two that had stepped over it looked at each other and snickered at me because I thought this Bible was such a big deal. No one in the house knew where it had come from. I asked the girl I came with if she knew whose it was, and she responded, "No hun, I've never seen it. Do you want to come back here with me?"

I told her, "Hold on." I walked over to the room of the owner of the house. As his face turned from his drawer of baggies, scales, and dope, I asked him, with a seriousness in my tone that he had to listen to, "Can I take this with me until the owner of it asks you for it, then I will bring it right back?"

"Sure, I don't care."

I gave him my number, then walked over to the girl I came with and told her I had to go because I had to get home for work in the morning. There was something with this Bible.

I drove the forty-five minutes back to my work apartment to find my room empty, with a single mattress in the middle of the floor. I sat down on that mattress and flipped open that Bible and read for hours. For the next couple days, I kept the Bible to myself in my room, comparing its translation with the New International Version I already had.

During these couple of days, I called that girl I took over there two or three times a day, and texted her the same amount. We'd had a good time for the past two weeks, and I was confused as to why she had stopped talking to me. On the third day, I was sitting at the small desk I had put together in my room for study and my computer when I got a call from her.

"Hey," I answered. "Are you okay?"

"Kind of. Not really," she replied with a soft tone, as if she had been crying for days. "You remember the guy that owned the house we were all at the other night?"

"Yeah, of course," I answered with a puzzled look only I could feel.

"Well, about twenty minutes after you left that night, he took a shot and had a heart attack in the middle of the living room floor. I was trying to do CPR, but he was dead when the paramedics arrived. They tried to revive him, but he died in the middle of the living room floor."

"Oh my goodness, I am so sorry!" I said to her, as my eyes turned immediately behind me to the Bible that I had found in that exact spot.

I'm walkin' around town, lookin' for ice to pick.
I'm skimmin' my pockets and gettin' nothin' but lint.

I spent my last dime, and then I spent a little more.
Last year was workin' on a 700 credit score!

Tore my roof down, life caved all around,
I set it on fire, thoughts are backwards now.

Historically speaking, I'm living misery lyrically while I'm presently
writing and then deleting what I'm reading.
Feeding the evil within me, thoughts are what he's eating!
Seemingly pleasing buffet when it's silent and I'm thinking!

I'm living in this paradox while trying to be a paragon.
I need a conscious shift I call the demon Ramadan.

I took deep breaths, and I counted to ten,
Again and again, but my mind is closed circuit.

Reminiscing on the past is the only thing that makes it last,
I try to slow it down and ground, but my mind is too fast.

All my memories have turned to boulders on my chest.
I've always wanted more, but never given it my best.

I'm so emotional, sometimes I lose control.
Sometimes I let 'em go, I'm so confused though.

Death is a lingering, breathing being following in my psyche.
Recovery to recovered, RELAPSE! Screw it, still recovering.

Dead friends join with and give me their experience.
My life is led by an old soul and messed-up head!

They always tell me home is where the heart is.
Tell me where a zombie lays walking dead and heartless!

FROM CHAINS TO SAVED

I write too many letters starting: Dear Departed,
Infinite pages saying statements, "sorry what I did!"

Silence in a room filled with people conversating.
Believe me when I try to leave it's hard for me to breathe!

Learned to pinch my inner thigh, cuz I couldn't cut me.
Pain is humanity—up—what're we discussing?

Death is but a dream and this life is our lucidity.
God created me, so creativity is divinity.

If you could see through my eyes and feel my empathy,
You'd take the cotton out your ears and try listening.

My Will will be the predicate, so mind you must subject to it.
My Will will be the predicate, so mind you must subject to it.

Searching for my blessing, looking for someone to help with it.
Speaking to the mirror, but unable to reflect with it!

When you lend your ear, I give you my heart.
I break that mirror just to cut it out with the shards!

Dark bathroom light creeping underneath the door,
Locked me in, feeling burning underneath the floor!

I'm screwed up from the neck up, wondering when all this will let up.
Step up, one eye fits that piece of mirror saying seven years!

Support is coming at me now from a lot of different angles.
I'd rather mess it all up than be held really accountable.

Changed my mind but now my hurdles looking insurmountable.
No human answers working searching in my Bible . . .

LEGION

MY FRIEND KATIE AND I were driving back to her house in Laurel, Montana, after an adventure of some sort. Me, the self-proclaimed physically-attractive, excitingly-rambunctious, overly-extroverted and energetic male Aquarius number three; her, the beautiful, tall, blue-eyed blonde, excitingly-rambunctious, comedically-combative, overly-extroverted Aquarius number two. Our pair was a force to be reckoned with in any social circle we entered. We had a ton of adventures, including four-wheeling, twisting donuts on side country roads, partying in bars, trips to cabins, and softball games with epic endings. We also had a darker side to our friendship, which included a lot of drug use. This particular day, we were driving back from picking up oxycodone 30s from a friend who was paralyzed from an accident. We were having our usual in-depth conversation about the meaning of it all as we pulled up to her house in her 2017 Tahoe.

As we pulled into her driveway, I could see past her house's pale green exterior, into a window that led to her living room and back into her kitchen. Standing at the window was the outline of a tall, dark man. As the rear tires bumped up the curb onto the driveway, the figure turned around and walked through the living room, into the kitchen, and vanished like smoke.

I turned to Katie and asked, "Who's in your house?"

She threw the car in park and looked at me with wide eyes, exclaiming, "You saw him?"

"Yeah. Something just walked from your window, through your kitchen."

She immediately began crying and put her face down into her hands.

"Katie," I continued, "What's up?"

"This thing has been following me since I was fifteen. No one has ever seen it before, and I don't ever talk about it." The crying continued behind her paling blue eyes.

"Well, it's time to talk about it. I'm not afraid of it. I'll go in there and kick it out right now."

This moment reminded me of the story in the Bible when Jesus meets Legion. Even in the middle of my drug addiction, I always knew the Power in the name of Jesus, and this was my first opportunity to utilize it in real life. I wanted to jump on it.

"He has been following me since I was fifteen, when I brought him out of a psychic circle board. It's like a Ouija board. A bunch of friends and I did a ritual with it, and he has been following me ever since."

"Do you know his name?"

"Yes. I never say it. Ugh, I'm getting sick. I can't say his name."
She continued crying.

I tell her, "It's okay. I'm going to go kick him out, then I'll come
get you."

She handed me the keys before I stepped out of the car. I stuck
my chest in the air like I was about to go approach a bully. I
walked up the brick steps of the porch, to her front door, and
put the keys in. My shoulders got heavy, and I began to feel the
pressure of some sort of dark presence. I turned the knob and
took a step in. I could smell him. The smell of a dark spirit is
only describable as a flat smell of death. It is distinct from any
other smell in the world that I have experienced, and this was the
first time I had it hit my nostrils plain as day, with a convicting
originality.

"Hey!" I yelled out as I took my second step into the house.
"You know why I am in here." I continued stepping through the
entryway to the right, into the living room. "I know who you are,
and you are not welcome here!"

I felt something come across my face like a gust of wind, and the
hair on the back of my neck stood up as the stench of death
became even stronger. I immediately dropped to my knees and
clasped my hands in prayer, proclaiming, "In the Name of Jesus,
I command you to leave this house!"

I felt a weight pressing down on my shoulders and back, as if
something was trying to push me into the floor in submission. I
tried again, "In the Name of Jesus, I command you to leave this
house! You are not welcome here!" The weight began to make

51

my lungs feel like they were collapsing, and I started to feel fear. Doubts crept into my mind with thoughts like, "You thought this would work? You thought you were strong enough to do this? You can't do this. He is too strong for you! You don't have any training! You are so stupid! This is so stupid!"

I couldn't get a grip of what was going on in my head and in my body. I thought for sure having the confidence of the Lord on my side would make this process super-simple. I had read plenty of stories about this being done all over the world, and here I was, in the middle of a living room on the wood floor, feeling like I was completely inadequate and stupid for even trying. I couldn't go back outside with my tail tucked between my legs, but I was beginning to feel like I was stupid for even trying this.

I tried one last time. "I command you to leave, in the name of Jesus!" I tried to bring myself up, but it felt like my heart was being tugged out of my chest toward the floor and my knees were stuck to it with superglue. I could tell the physical feeling of being stuck was coming straight from the unseen world. The powerlessness of that moment was a scary feeling. I didn't know what to do. I had tried the name of Jesus and commanding it out like all the books I had read and stories I had heard, but the smell was circling around me and a boulder was being put on my back.

"Jesus," I said, calling to Him for help, "I need . . ." Immediately, the weight began to be lifted off me, and I could breathe again, ". . . Your help. Jesus expel evil from this house. Holy Spirit, come down and enter this house, that nothing may be here except You." I felt tingling course from my heart, through my body, and it flew out of me and into the house. I was experiencing the Holy Spirit coming from inside my heart and flowing into this house, expelling evil. The smell was instantly gone. The weight that had been on me turned into a feeling like

I was floating from within. I stood up as if being helped from the ground and smiled. "Wow, God." I said. "That was cool!"

I walked out to the car, where Katie was still sitting in tears, and told her, "We're good. Come on in."

"What do you mean? What did you do?"

"Jesus kicked him out."

"There is no way." Her eyes teared up again, and her face went into her hands.

I reached out with my hand on her shoulder, and she looked at me with her glowing, magnified eyes. "Katie, for real. He is gone. Out of the house. I promise you. He can't come back while I'm here."

We went inside, and I proceeded to move past that experience without explaining it to her. We went straight into using the drugs we had just gone and picked up.

Sprayin' and Prayin'

KATIE HAD A SOFTBALL TEAM she managed, or coached, or whatever it's called when you lead a beer league team, and they needed another male player. We were running late to the game, so she was driving fast down the highway. We began noticing it wasn't a cloudy sky we were watching develop—it was smoke.

I looked over to where the fire was coming from and could see the flames on the nearest mountain to us. This was my first time experiencing a natural disaster this close. My immediate thought, which came out in a statement, was, "I wonder if there is something we can do to help?"

Katie had her daughter with us, and I was not used to riding with a four-year-old girl in the back of the car, so my call to action fell on deaf ears.

We went to the softball game. I played center field and made three great plays. I hit a three-run homerun, and a walk-off game-winning double in the last inning. We were all very excited and getting ready to go to the after-game get-together. For some reason, I had the thought to ride with a different girl than Katie. We were all going to the same place, and I think I was wanting to show off one of my new raps to her.

We were less than five minutes into the drive—and less than a minute into my rapping—when her phone would not stop blowing up. She answered to learn that her parents' house was directly in the path of the fire and was being evacuated by the family. She was trying to decide whether she should drive over there or not, because the police had blockaded the road and were not letting people in anymore. She was worried about her boat and fifth wheel parked over there. I told her not to worry about the blockade, and that we would get through it.

Five minutes later, and driving directly at a cloud of black smoke, we arrived at the blockade. The young officer did a great job with his duties, but also understood the importance that we get by, so he let us with the heeded warning to move fast because it was coming right here. When we got to the house, there were roughly eight people helping move things out of the three-to four-bedroom trailer home, with an older woman, grandma, sitting on the porch with her cane. Everyone was in a frenzy as I walked by, attempting quick introductions while asking for anything I could do to help. The frenzy everyone was in kinda left me loned-out, so I looked around . . .

They had set all of their hoses up with sprinklers on them around the entire yard to stop the fire. The efficiency of this tactic did not seem very helpful for a fire barreling down on us, but it gave me an idea. I can't really remember if I read this somewhere, learned it somewhere, or if I was just given the idea at that moment, but I felt like I knew exactly what to do to protect that house. I saw a vision of the fire consuming everything around the house, but it was still standing, unharmed. I quickly moved into action and asked the person nearest to me whose house this was before getting permission to unscrew a sprinkler head and use the hose. I knew how to spray a house really well from my training in the pest control industry. All the skills I have developed throughout life have never become obsolete.

I looked up before I began to see the thickest, darkest, most hellish smoke covering the sky, followed by a red-hot fire as far as I could see in the near distance; all backed by wind blowing directly at us. I began by spraying the entire fence line between the house and the fire, front and back, to make it no longer flammable. I made a moat around the bottom of the fence, and sprayed any trees I thought had a chance of a spark igniting. I sprayed the house as if every millimeter was a potential fire hazard, and made a moat around the bottom of it. I sprayed the decks, over and under. The entire time I was spraying, I was praying, "Please keep this house safe. Please don't let the fire come here. Please protect this house, if it does. Let no harm come to this house. Protect this house, God. Protect this house, God."

I took the hose around the opposite side of the house, and began the process quickly. After I had completed my first full lap, the man of the house stopped me and said, "Young man, thank you!" I was so wrapped up in my job and talking with God that I hadn't noticed everyone was watching me spraying and praying as they were evacuating the house. No one could hear me, but they could feel me.

I took my hose and my God and ran to the other side of the house, where I had originally started. I kept my eyes down on the house as I made a lap for my moat. Before beginning on the fence, I wanted to check how much time we had, so I looked up. At some point during the spraying and praying, the wind had completely shifted in the opposite direction, and I could no longer see flames or black smoke, just distant white and grey smoke. I dropped the hose and threw my hands up in praise and thanksgiving! I was amazed at my God. I then went and congregated with the neighborhood people, who had begun to calm from the frenzy. I didn't share the experience I had had with God with anyone there. I let everyone have their time. I went straight home and wrote it in my journal, to be able to share at such a time as this. My journals and God soon became the last things I had that my addiction hadn't taken from me . . .

Open-Minded
and Willing

I HAD MADE IT TWENTY-SIX days without any drugs while living in the Montana Rescue Mission. It had not been easy. I had been drinking alcohol to calm my nerves every couple days, but I had made it without drugs for the second-longest amount of time in my life since I was twelve years old. I was going to two twelve-step meetings a day, along with anything else I could find in the community that would help me connect to spirituality. According to everything I had learned through experiences or other people's wisdom, that was my only hope of getting out of this mess I was in.

Here were some of the things I was doing:

— Twelve-step meetings

— Buddhist meditations

— Tai Chi

— Oneness meditations

— Bible studies

— Church

— Outpatient programs at the treatment center

— The MMA gym

— Dropping in unannounced at the probation office

— Programs at the rescue mission

— Meeting with addicts outside of twelve-step rooms

— Making solemn oaths never to use again

— Drinking only, and no drugs

— Drugs only, and no drinking

— Cutting everyone out of my life

— Making a bunch of new friends to have in my life

— Anything I saw that might be able to help me stop using

---

*I was still unable to grasp something
that calmed the nerves inside of me.*

Then I heard about a recovery get-together at the park down the street from the Mission that was going to have games, food, and a speaker who had two PhDs in fields related to psychology and recovery. When I asked other people in the community about this event, they told me it was kind of a big deal that this guy was coming to speak. I decided to walk down and jump in to learn, like I was open to doing with anything during this season in my life.

There were well over 200 people there—closer to 300, I would say. There was a cornhole tournament, barbecue, and a bunch of different companies there that were sponsoring the event and marketing themselves as outlets for addicts. This event was not affiliated with any twelve-step fellowship, government agency, church, or anything like that. From what I remember, it was just an event put on to play games and listen to this man speak.

After I played some games and danced around with a group of people during a native drum circle, I went over to the picnic benches and chairs set up by a makeshift stage. I don't really remember how it came about, but I ended up talking to the director of the whole event and told her about a poem I had written that would fit the event and the idea of addiction awareness well. I ended up performing the poem at the microphone in front of the crowd right before this man got up to speak. You can see the poem on my Facebook page, Adam Vibe Gunton, or if you are on a device, here: http://bit.ly/WeDoRecover

I released it for my one year clean/sober date, November 6, 2018.

I went back to my seat while everyone was still clapping and cheering, and the director came up to the microphone and said, "Wow! That was truly amazing. Thank you for sharing that with us. All right, that was a great opening for our guest speaker. He has two PhDs—one in clinical psychology, and one in philosophy. Please help me welcome . . ." I am keeping his name anonymous because of what I am about to share of my experience with this man.

61

For the next hour, this man taught about the spirituality related to addiction and the planet. Everyone was fixated on him as he shared that each organism on the planet has its own spirit attached to it. "There is a spirit of the aspen tree. There is a spirit of this park bench. A spirit of the grass you are standing on, and, yes, a spirit to each substance that people are using." He went on to share about how much trauma is attached to the spirit of cocaine due to the amount of war, addiction, greed, and death associated with every kilo that gets into the hands of the user. He explained that this spirit is very large, and is with every addict who has ever used cocaine.

"Why do you think liquor is called spirits?" he continued. "And just think about the ceremonial way you go up to a bar to give your penance, money, confess what spirits you want, and then give your offering to the bartender. You are inviting the spirit of alcohol into your life at that moment and allowing it to begin to take control of your body."

'Wow,' I thought. 'This makes a ton of sense.'

"Now," he began, as he turned his shoulders to address the entire crowd with his next statement, "You have come under an agreement with the spirit of the substance you are addicted to. To break that agreement, you must start another agreement between yourself and that spirit, and break the bond it has on you to use it. Right now, it has a hold of you. You must speak to it as if it is your friend, and tell it you no longer invite it into your life with that substance, but that you invite it into your life for something else."

'This is making way more sense than it should,' I continued thinking in my head, 'But what if . . .' My hand shot up in the air

62

so quick and high that the entire crowd looked toward me, causing him to pause his thought and turn to me.

"Yes? A question?" He took a couple steps towards me.

"Yeah," I began. "Let's say, hypothetically, you have accidentally made agreements with all kinds of spirits. Like, the spirit of cocaine, the spirit of crack, the spirit of heroin, the spirit of alcohol, the spirit of meth, the spirits of greed, lust, lying, depression, anxiety, and many more . . . Isn't there One, All-Powerful, All-Knowing and King-of-All-the-Spirits that you could go to that will break the agreements with all these other spirits you have made agreements with?"

The whole crowd gasped, and I heard multiple comments come up from the crowd, "Ooooooo, that's a good question!"

He was taken aback by the question. Noticing the crowd wanted an answer, he replied, "Yes. But the only One who has ever been able to accomplish that was Jesus, right?"

I nodded as I noticed people in the crowd's thoughts begin to spin, turning their heads back to him as he continued his teaching.

I was not all-too-wise at this time to the reality of the spiritual ramifications of what he was teaching. I actually thought what he was teaching was really cool. At that point in my life, I was giving every teacher around me (even addicts that just had a little clean time) authority over my mind, and gave them the right to implant beliefs within me. I just wanted to be free from addiction. That was all I wanted, and I was willing to do or believe whatever it took to make that happen.

After he had finished his speech, everyone went back to eating, playing games, and socializing with each other. I went over to one of the booths and was talking with some ladies who worked for a local nonprofit when I felt a tap on my shoulder. I turned to lock eyes with a young woman who worked for the speaker. "Dr. ... wants to meet with you. He is granting you a mini-session with him." She pointed about half-a-football-field away to a gazebo, where I could faintly see him sitting in a chair, with his back turned to us and an empty chair in front of him.

'Wow, cool!' I thought.

"Thank you! Right now?" I asked, with wide eyes of excitement.

"Yes. He is waiting for you."

"Sweet!" I finished, with my first steps toward him.

I walked over to him, and the noise of the event drowned out softer and softer until all I heard was a dull wind. I felt it as I took the first of four steps up underneath the concrete gazebo with the blue top. A midday shadow cast perfectly over our meeting place, showing light all around us, but a perfect darkness in our space. He was stiff-backed and looking away from me without moving, as if he was meditating. I sat down at the chair across from him with a smile of excitement and anticipation, and began to notice a calm darkness about him. His sunglasses cast a small shadow underneath his eyes, yet there was no light coming from anywhere that could cause it. I looked past this, and stuck out my hand with my usual passionate delivery. "Hi! I'm Adam Gunton."

His hand reached out, and as it touched mine, there was a coldness coming from it that was weird on such a hot summer day—but some people just have cold hands, right?

"Nice to meet you, Adam. You are incredibly talented. I really enjoyed your poem. I wanted to get to know you a little bit, and what is going on in your life."

"Well, I have twenty-six days right now." He interrupted with the usual *congratulations* before I continued. "I believe I am here for a really big purpose. I want to help millions of people. There is something inside of me that makes people automatically comfortable with me. I tend to connect with people quickly, and what I have been experiencing lately is people sharing their deepest and darkest traumas with me. It is taking a toll on me, hearing these things I am hearing. There is a lot of childhood trauma that people share with me that they have never shared with anyone else. Some of the things I am experiencing are frickin' crazy, too. I'm seeing a psychologist right now, and I am afraid to tell her anything else because she has to diagnose me with something to be able to keep working with me and be paid by insurance. She is throwing the word schizophrenia around."

He interrupted me. "You do not have schizophrenia. I have dealt with many cases, and we would not be able to have the conversation we are having if you did."

"Thank you. I know I don't, and that I am not crazy, and that these things are real. What do I do?"

"Well," he began, "You believe in Jesus?"

"Yes," I replied.

"Then there is a way to take all the emotions and trauma and pass it through you to Him. When you are listening to these stories from these people, envision Jesus is standing behind you. Open your heart to receive for them, and as all their hurt, emotions, and traumas pass through your heart, envision them going directly into Jesus standing behind you."

---

*Guard your heart with all vigilance,
for from it are the sources of life.*
Proverbs 4: 23 NET

*But you, LORD, are a shield that protects me:
you are my glory and the One who restores me.*
Psalm 3:3 NET

Like I said, at this time, I was listening to everyone's advice as if it were true without knowing the dangerous spiritual implications of allowing all these spirits of trauma and pain to come directly into my heart. I was ignorant to the fact that not everyone is on the good side of the spiritual battle.

He continued, "I was telling you, along with the crowd, that there is a spirit to everything on this planet. You can talk to them. You can work with them. You seem more advanced with your spiritual walk, so I am going to give you a couple secrets."

I leaned in with excitement and an itching ear. Just then, I witnessed as the shadow beneath his glasses manifested three-dimensionally and grew out of his face, revealing an evil spirit within him. It looked like a skeleton made of black smoke that I could see through to the man's face. The spirit showed its entire face, in front of his, for half a second before returning inside of him. "The spirits love when you talk to them. You can ask them for anything you want, and they will help you get it. They are hungry, and they are thirsty. Whenever you eat, thank them for being in your life, and take a little pinch of your food before you eat and set it next to your plate for them, and tell them it is for them. But the thing they love the most is water. They are very thirsty. The best thing to do to get them to work for you is to open your bottle of water, take a sip of it, then leave it open and set it to the side. Offer it to them and do not take another drink of it. Ask them for whatever you want."

When an unclean spirit goes out of a person, it passes through waterless places looking for rest but not finding any . . .

Luke 11:24 NET

As soon as our conversation was finished, I went back over to the table where I had been sitting, grabbed my backpack, and said my quick goodbyes to the people I had met. I walked straight to the Crystal Lounge Casino with my last twenty dollars and sat down at the Texas hold'em poker table. I got a bottle of water with my twenty dollars in chips, opened it, and took a sip. I placed it next to me with the cap off and said under my breath where no one could hear me, "Spirit of gambling, this is for you. Let's see what you got." My first hand was ten-three off suit, a hand you should almost always fold with. I went all-in and had two callers who had more money behind them to play the rest of the hand. The flop came ten, ten, three. I was sold.

POSSESSION

I'm sitting down to write this piece to share the things I bottle deep,
So possibly my skin will peel, revealing bones I turn to keys.
And if you're one that's listening, I'm not searching for your belief,
Because I'm doing this for me, I call it my reality . . .

I'm witness to the war that rages on in all the air we breathe.
So focusing is hard for me while hearing all these gnashing teeth!
The undertaking, revelating, how to lead's what I'm debating.
Sure success I hope to do but certain to the things I see!

It seems to be that presently I'm seeking for my true beliefs.
Not speaking philosophically, I know Christ is my God and King,
But recently, while on my knees, I'm crying with apologies,
Because I hear Him calling me but can't step with integrity!

If you're wondering where love went, maybe you should seek within.
You're yelling out for help from God, but refusing relationship!
It proves the kind of state you're in, assessing all your closest friends,
Then cutting almost all of them to feel a little progress.

Changing different ways, my pain is leaving day-by-day.
I know that God is with me even when I'm speaking Satan's name.
While He's communicating, habits are debilitating.
Responsibility's on me for eating off the burning plate.

I see things creeping in your stares, you're having fun while unaware.
The eyes attached to you deceived by thoughts you have subconsciously,
But offering my knowledge makes these demons want my company,
Cuz knowing that I'm heavenly, they share the depths of hell with me.

I claim this page as saved for rage to play with ways I motivate.
I state my anger is controlled, but art's driven by rented souls.
Not pissed at who I am but what I am, due to the things I do.
Confused how I can choose to lose when I'm one of the chosen few!

This section is aggression coming out of my depression.
When I can't move out of bed, the world is weighing around my neck,
The future is so far away, and seconds are my failed success,
I count to ten and breathe in deep but all I hear is hopelessness.

What causes fights and quarrels, if not from your own desires?
Right now I'm boasting evil, so I'm witnessing the fire.
Teaching things to demons, might as well be preaching to the choir.
Got an offer but won't sell eternity to Satan's buyers!

Higher higher higher higher, anchor's lifting, wind is shifting.
Drifted off the path again, decision's mine and soul is His.
I'm wrestling Goliath of our times in this addiction.
I am David with the Truth, and faith in God will pin the fiction.

The rain didn't bother me as I was speedily walking the two miles from the Montana Rescue Mission to MSU Billings, where the oneness meditation event was taking place. I was so dead-set on my recovery and achieving my thirty days clean that my mind had nothing going on in it except the worship music blaring in my headphones. As I came around a curve to Poly Street, hugging my own body with determination, a small, black compact car without a front bumper started pulling up to me and flashing its brights. I stood up tall and squinted into the windshield to see a friend—someone I had used with and recorded music with in his grandma's basement—waving his black cotton glove-covered hand at me to get in the car. I thought twice because I knew our history, but something felt right about getting in with him. I opened the passenger side door and hopped in.

The first thing I heard when I got in the car was the same worship song I was just listening to in my headphones! "If you've got chains! He's a chain breaker!" as he said, "What's up? What the heck are you doing out here in the rain?"

I was dumbfounded by the song being on in his car. I was listening to Pandora, so there was no way for us to be on the same radio station or anything. We must have been on some type of frequency together, though. "Dude!" I exclaimed. "I was just listening to that song when you pulled up! You are definitely supposed to be here. Thanks for picking me up."

"Well, what're you doing out here in the rain?" he asked with a little grin behind his Morpheus-looking prescription sunglasses.

"I'm headed to the college for a oneness meditation seminar. Do you want to come?" After explaining briefly what I knew about oneness meditation meet-ups (which was clearly nothing at all, as you will see shortly), he decided to join me.

We were only a few tenths-of-a-mile from our destination, so we didn't have a lot of time to get together for small talk. We parked in the parking lot and walked around the campus, looking for the correct building between all these old castle-like brick structures. When we found the right one, it seemed like the steps I was taking to the door were that of a medieval time period. I walked up to the big wood door and went through. I felt like I was walking up the stairs in Bowser's castle, with Ryan right behind me.

As we walked in, we had to walk up another small set of stairs surrounded by rock walls that opened up into a large room like one where the Knights Templar would convene. It seemed like the wood floor of the room stretched on forever. As we walked to the other side, the picture became clearer of three couches in a U shape, facing a fireplace with a burning fire. In front of the fire sat a small woman, alone, in her own comfy chair, with her eyes closed. A small speaker next to her was playing soft eastern meditation music. Right as we got to the area of the couches, she opened her eyes, gaze fixed directly on me.

"Hello," she said with a gentle and inviting tone.

"Hello," I replied with much more of a caveman confidence tone. "I'm here for the oneness meditation."

She smiled, looked at Ryan, looked back at me, and said, "You must be Adam. Who is your friend?"

At this time, Ryan was already catching a weird feeling about the environment, pacing around the place, feeling the energies. I was oblivious. "Hi, I'm Ryan. Nice to meet you."

"Hello, Ryan. Welcome." As she said that, another woman arrived—the one I had met a week previous at the spiritual gift shop for a meditation meeting. She was a beautiful, tall and slender woman in her late forties or early fifties. She had short, dark hair and piercing blue eyes behind thin-framed glasses. Today she was wearing a purple long-sleeved shirt over a black undershirt. Purple, my favorite color. It was as if this woman was there to bring me in.

I smiled and stepped toward her with my arms out for a hug, pulling her in close with our hearts connected, as we did the week before. The warmth of the hug made me feel so comforted and peaceful.

"Mmmmm . . . you are such a wonderful hugger," she said with a flattering voice from my left shoulder.

As I let go and turned to introduce her to Ryan, another young woman walked up and took her seat on the couch to the left of the little leader lady by the fire. "Hey. Hey. Hey," was all she said. It was three women, Ryan, and I, sitting in a circle of couches and a chair in front of a fire. Ryan was next to the last woman on the couch directly across from me.

The leader started off with a description of the beliefs of this group. "Everyone is one, we are all one, we are all love, and we are all god."

At this point of my life, I was so spiritually willing to do anything I think might help me, that I didn't even think twice about making this confession. I didn't even notice as Ryan began looking around this group with a "Nope!" undertone. He was dressed in all-black everything, from the beanie, to the glasses, to the gloves. He looked like the darkest character in the room, but looks can be deceiving.

We began to do different types of ritualistic meditation practices. Things I had done variations of before in my own practices, but never guided. We did breathing techniques with our eyes closed while thinking about things we love and people we love, while sending that love around the world to them. My close friend Sean came into my heart, and I meditated on sending him love during this.

I am breaking from the book to give warning. At this point of writing this story, I am sitting at my computer desk with my tea remembering this story vividly, and the whole experience I had leading up to one of the most intense and harmful spiritual attacks I have experienced to this day. I just received a random message in my phone inviting me to a workshop tomorrow night for something of the same type of New Age energy healing meditation practice. Needless to say, we have free will and must guard our hearts with the spiritual wisdom we gain in this life.

I was all smiles during this whole part of the workshop. I love love. I love loving people. I love loving things. I love loving God. I love loving everything. This part was easy for me to do. I was just unaware of the spiritual immaturity I was practicing as I stood up to begin singing *Om nama Shivaya*. It's right around this time that Ryan said, "I've got to go help a friend move," and walked out of the building. He told me later that he was very aware of this being against what Jesus teaches.

The leader told me to "Stand up and close your eyes. Wrap your arms around yourself and give yourself a warm hug. Tell yourself you love yourself. Now sway with the music, and sing at your own pace with her." As I opened my heart to this, as soon as I opened my mouth to begin chanting with them, I started to feel a tingling sensation in the bottom of my spine. Right as I felt that begin, I heard her soft voice say, "Feel the sensation of the love entering into you." I wasn't getting freaked out, but more and more open to the spiritual experience as the tingling continued up my spine and into my neck. When it reached the back of my head, I was in a trance and swaying my body like waves, to the left and right, inviting anything to come into me that wanted to. She told us to open our eyes.

I was having a little different experience within myself. I was feeling at ease, comforted, at peace, and serene. I was enjoying it very much, and sat down onto the couch. I felt as though I melted into it to listen to her continue her workshop. A conversation arose about Jesus being my Lord and Savior. I was unlearned in the Bible and had not been reading it for long, at this time, so confessing my belief was as far as I could go.

She said, "I love Jesus. He was a master teacher and ascended master. I have a beautiful picture of Him. Look at Him." I remember being in a dream-like state, leaning over to look at her phone of a painting of Jesus with sparkles coming from his green eyes and white skin. It looked like Jesus, but had a different feel to it.

As I nodded at the picture and began to lean back into my couch, her eyes fixed with a piercing brown stare straight into mine. Then she said something about Jesus' brother's story. The statement confused me so much that I turned my head to the side with an eyebrow raised and began to nod as she giggled, acting like I knew what she was talking about. Then she opened her mouth wider, with a deeper laugh, and turned her head to the left toward the woman on the other couch. At this moment, although her face turned away from mine, another face stayed in the same position, staring at me with a laugh. It was a shadow with dark eyes and a dark mouth that was a greyish-green color of smoke taking up the body. I saw it for less than an instant before I felt as though something hit me in the head. Not like a physical punch to the head, but like the aftereffects of that punch. I noticed a ringing in my ears and saw lights quickly overtake my peripherals before coming back into focus, yet very confused.

She was still giggling and turned back to me and said, "Come here. I want to do something." She motioned with her hand to follow her as she stood up and walked the opposite direction of me, between both the other couches where the other two women were sitting. She walked me over to a mirror on the wall.

"Take a look at yourself. Aren't you handsome? Tell yourself you love yourself." She pinched my cheek, and as I looked in the mirror, it was a very unfamiliar reflection coming back at me. I was there and aware, but I had a massive amount of confusion as to what exactly was going on. My reflection smiled and said, "I love you," looking into my eyes. She hugged me real tight and giggled, before leading me back to the couches.

One of the women, the one on the couch directly across from me, told everyone it was time that she had to go. She got up, bid everyone a good day, and walked out. We continued chatting for another few minutes, then she ended the session and brought me and the other woman to the kitchen, where there was a whole bunch of food prepared. Hors d'oeuvres of fruit, cheese, crackers, and other various snacks were laid out on a table for us to enjoy. We all made plates before going to sit down together at a table. She put a video on her phone of an Indian speaker who was talking about some kind of spiritual practice. After finishing my plate, I really felt the need to get out of there. I was not feeling right and just wanted to go.

I gave the two ladies hugs and gave them sentiment of love and gratitude before walking out the door of this large castle-like building. The moment I stepped out of the building, I shot outside and to the right of my body. I witnessed myself for the next thirty-six hours doing all the things I had sworn I wasn't going to do; all the things I had been working so hard for the past four weeks not to do.

When I say I went outside of my body, it was the most unusual experience I had had to this point of my life. I was able to see through my eyes, but at the same time—almost in flashes of momentary perception change—I would see myself from an angle of above my head, two or three feet, and to the right and back. It was like I was in the perspective of something else watching over me. I was no longer in control of my thoughts, though I was still aware of them. I had a thought that 'going to the casino with our last eighty dollars would be a great idea right now,' and before I could even have a second thought, my body was walking towards the casino.

I walked the two-and-a-half miles in a dream state, going inside and outside of my body all the way to the Gold Dust Casino, and sat down at the 2-6 limit hold'em poker game. Everyone in the place knew me, but it had been a couple months since I had been around. As I was sitting at the table, I took a sip of water and set it next to me, offering it to the spirits of gambling. I could feel heavy conviction from the battle going on within me at this moment, and could hear the Spirit telling me how blasphemous this practice was, but I was still not in control of what I was doing. I put all eighty dollars down on the table. I remember feeling a sort of depression overwhelming me, a sense of heaviness without any sort of comfort. I was still going in and out of this perspective of watching myself doing what I was doing. The dealer, who had known me for a couple years at this point, leaned over in the middle of a hand and whispered to me, "Hey, are you okay?" I remember getting a jolt of energy, sitting up quickly in my chair, and nodding violently with a crazy smile. She nodded softly back with a concerned look in her eyes.

Going back and talking with people who witnessed these things after they had run their course was as much a trip as it was during the experiences. Being able to hear the perspective of others who witnessed this chapter of my life has greatly benefitted my willingness to speak out about what was really going on. The people that were there, that saw the way I acted, and felt the way I felt in a space, have since assured me that they were aware of something very weird going on, as well. As much as I wish I didn't need the approval or stamp from other people that I am not crazy, it helps when other people see and back up these stories, too.

I was there for less than ten minutes before I looked down at my stack and had thirty dollars in chips left. Again, a thought crossed my mind of, 'you can go get a twenty and have enough left over to get a needle.' Before I had a second thought, I was picking up my chips without saying bye, and cashing them out while on my phone unblocking a girl on Facebook who could help me pick up. At first, when I messaged her, she was excited to hear from me, but asked me about my decision to quit a few weeks ago. I quickly moved past this, as I always did in this situation, and began walking the over three miles to the west end where she was. I remember being out of my body for this entire walk. I was experiencing something talking to me in my head and laughing at me for what we were going to do. It was as if something was inside of me and inside of my head, controlling my body and laughing at my consciousness.

I got to the other side of town and picked up from this girl who was always excited to see me. I had planned it out that she would bring a needle with her that I would buy from her for five dollars. After getting the dope from her, I realized neither of us had water. I looked across the street and saw a soda vending machine sitting outside a closed store. I ran across the street and walked up to the vending machine, excited to be taking my last step towards getting these drugs in my system. I looked up and down the drink selection and was upset that there was no water. I heard a small voice in my heart say, "This is how I try and protect you . . ."

I heard the laughter in my head again as I looked up and down the selection and came to a conscious choice that Mountain Dew was going to be my best option to mix this up with and put in my vein. I put the $1.25 in the machine, and as I went to push the button for Mountain Dew, I noticed that the beverage right above it was water.

"What the heck?" I thought, before the small voice in my heart said, "This is how I try to protect you . . ."

The laughing in my head continued, and I shook my head in amazement and pushed the button to release the water. It was jammed. "This is how I try and protect you . . ." The voice in my heart was a little louder this time. Laughter in my head got louder as I pushed hard with my thumb until the water released, but when it got to the bottom, it got stuck before falling. "This is how I try and protect you . . .!" The voice in my heart was beginning to get very stern, and the laughter was very loud in my head.

I reached in the machine and began feeling around and pushing around until the water came down where I was able to grab onto it. It had me. The evil inside me had taken over my ability to choose whether or not I was going to do this. The pathway was about to open to another evil that would introduce itself to everyone I had been working to grow relationship with for months. I was kicked out of the homeless shelter by the end of the next day. I lost friendships with people who were counting on me, and embarrassed myself with a crazy fiasco in a cafeteria. I was about to go down a path of uncontrollable darkness I had not yet experienced.

I was sitting in Veronica's car, alone, crying with my Bible in my hand. Then the thing inside of me started telling me I should kill myself. That would be the best option. I could leave this fight and wouldn't have to go through any of this anymore. I would even get to wake up and be with Jesus and out of the fight! I opened my Bible, and within five minutes I had found eight verses that my mind put together in such a way that corroborated my thoughts of being able to kill myself and go to heaven.

'I'm doing it. Tonight,' I thought, as the tears began to settle on this absolute decision. My thoughts were spinning in such a way that they sounded like my own, but, looking back, I know they weren't. All the sudden, that feeling hit me again. That feeling of absenteeism. My body had just lost the Spirit, and fear gripped my entire body. 'No. This is wrong,' I thought, 'I need help. I can't kill myself.'

I began texting Jonathon, one of the leaders at my church, telling him the thoughts I was having. As I began texting him, the Spirit began filling back into my body. It was like, the faith in reaching out was enough for the Spirit to come back into my presence. I sent the text, and he called me right away. A short talk was enough to get me out of the state I was in, and he told me to read Galatians and Ephesians. To this point, I had never read these books in the Bible.

I went inside to Veronica's basement and sat on one of the couches while she sat on the other. She was such a good friend to me, and was the last one I really had at that time that stuck by me. I told her what my elder had just told me to do, and asked her if she would like me to read it out loud for both of us. She agreed, and I opened up to Ephesians.

For the next hour or two, with Veronica sitting on the couch opposite the couch I was sitting on, we witnessed as a demon screamed and yelled at me and God, through me, as if it was me. I watched myself stand up after reading a chapter in the Bible, look up and scream at God, and tell Him how dumb that was. I was yelling profane things I have never been able to say in my entire life. I have never, since I was a small child, been able to say the Lord's Name in vain—just something I was born with. Whatever was inside of me that day screamed it into the sky and hit my chest.

I remember looking at the Bible, the Words on the page, and as I was coming up to a verse, the whole page would go blurry. I would close my eyes and pray, "God, I know I am supposed to see this. Please give me my sight." I would open my eyes and my sight was restored.

It is an intense experience watching yourself battling for yourself with something that's inside of yourself. The Bible was my only weapon. I remember screaming at Veronica and the sky saying, "Where the f*** does it say I can't cuss?" and the next verse I read was Ephesians 4:29. Veronica and I looked at each other, amazed. Veronica had about three years clean and sober at this time, and was able to witness this battle. She believes, fully, that it was a spiritual battle of Good and evil going on inside of her basement.

AHHHHH! DEAD!

IT WAS A FEW DAYS before Halloween, 2017, and I looked up from my worn-out shoes to find myself in the garage of my dope dealer's house. There was a fog of cigarette smoke above the motorcycles that had been taken apart, surrounding the circle of chairs put together in the back of the space. I was alone in the chairs. I was alone in my head. And I was alone in my soul. There were a few other people in the garage, standing among the motorcycle parts, and there was a frustrated energy pushing through the space from all of them.

"Shut up! Sit down and stop it!" my dope dealer yelled at his four-year-old son, who was running around with a costume knife, hitting people. Everyone in there was giving dirty looks to this poor kid as he bid for their attention.

"Ahhhhh! Dead!" he yelled as he hit one of the men standing there. The man gave him a dirty look, and looked at my dealer with a 'Put him away' look. The dealer leaned toward his son with an angry tone and the kid ran away, laughing out loud, hitting me on the shoulder while he passed me. "Dead!"

I smiled at him, unwilling to hate a kid for needing attention.

The boy stood about two arm's length away from me, staring at his mom and dad as they began to argue about what to do about the new dope they got from a new connect. "Well, try it out!" my dope dealer yelled at his wife.

"I don't want to be the first! It looks like soap!" she yelled back.

The dealer looked at me, and I shook my head before he was able to offer it to me. He turned back to his wife. "Just try it! The dude said it is really good." All the while, this four-year-old boy was watching, with his eyes moving back and forth from mom to dad.

He began to take steps towards his parents when I had a sense of The Spirit flow into me and desired to reach out to the kid. Before I could think about it or make my own decision, my hand reached out and lightly touched the boy on his shoulder. He looked at me with the knife clenched tightly in both hands, and as he began his swing to hit me, my eyes closed and my head bowed. He never finished his swing as I heard, from inside my heart, The Spirit begin to pray for this child's life. I heard my heart speaking life into him, love into him, understanding into him, and protection over him. I was not in control of what my heart was saying, and cannot even remember the exact words that were being said.

This only lasted about fifteen to twenty seconds, and was in total silence, but during this whole time, the kid stood there, stiff and without a peep. I felt The Spirit finish and leave me, and, as I opened my eyes to look back up at him, he was sitting down on the ground, looking directly into my eyes and placing the knife on the ground. He stared deeply into my eyes for what seemed like eternity, but was really only a few seconds. Then he stood up, without the knife, and walked around calmly the rest of the night. No more screaming, or hitting, or fighting for attention.

After his mother had tried the new dope and let us know it was safe and good, I bought my bag and headed back out to my hotel, knowing something significant had happened, but being too caught up in my addiction to think much more of it . . .

REFLECTION

NOVEMBER 6, 2017, I WAS in my hotel room, alone, in the darkest hour of my life. I had been beaten up by my addiction, time and time again, and I still had to continue using to make it through this day. I sat on the top of the toilet, shower to my left and mirror to my right, showing me what I had become in my peripheral. I prepared a shot from my bag of dope, and tied my arm off to shoot up. My veins were thick and ready to go. Something was preparing for a war within me that I will never forget.

My first attempt into a vein went right through it. I drew back and no blood poured in, which showed I was not in a vein. I heard something laugh at me in my head as I pulled it back out. Something in my heart told me, "Don't do this." I had heard this voice over and over and over again, but I had never been able to muster up the power to follow it. I stuck the needle back in my arm about a centimeter from the first attempt, which had begun releasing a small stream of blood down my arm. I felt like I was in the vein, but when I drew back, there was no blood; I missed again. I did not understand how I was missing, because the veins were so big and easy to get. So big that they were bleeding down my arm. As I pulled it out, that laugh in my head began again.

It was a chilling moment as I began to put the needle in my arm a third time and noticed, out of my peripheral, something in the mirror with me. A dark, shadowy figure that was within my own reflection. Something was inside of me in that reflection, and it was laughing at my attempts to shoot up, my only escape from this horrible reality of life I had brought myself to. I began to hear it say within my head, 'Hahahaha! You can't get the vein! You can't get it!' My eyes began to wallow up with tears. Tears of loneliness. Tears of all the things I had lost over my life. The relationships, the jobs, the family, the friends, the homes, the hope—and, in my mind, God.

I stuck my arm over ten times through my tattoos—a technique I used to not have to show my track marks to the world. My arm was bleeding from multiple places, and the blood was coming out so much that it had begun falling on the bathroom floor, as did my tears from my face. I heard another voice in my heart, 'Don't do this. I have already bled for you.'

I cried more, sticking myself again, having to push harder with the now-dull needle to make it past the skin. 'Hahahaha. You can't get it!' something in my mind said. I looked straight at myself in the mirror, and through the tears, I saw darkness. Pure darkness coming from my eyes, and a ghostly figure coming in and out of my face like the doctor at the park.

'You have to use the ol' reliable vein!' the voice in my head said, pointing my attention to the one vein on my other arm I never use because it is so obvious and not covered by tattoos. I took the tie off my left arm and put it around my right arm, fully aware there is something battling within me causing all this sadness, all this grief, and all this need for this drug.

'Get it,' it started. 'You are going to love this one. This will be amazing.' I heard it giggling at me.

I thought to myself, 'If I use this vein, everyone is going to know.'

'Everyone already knows you're a drug addict. No one believes in you. No one cares about you. No one even cares where you are right now. Just do it.' I put it directly into the vein with force, and then I was in. I drew back a pure, clean stream of blood, and an excitement ran over me.

As I began to push the contents back into my vein, I heard the Voice in my heart say, "Enough!" and the syringe clogged, stuck with my thumb pressing against the end.

I pushed harder, trying to get it to go in my vein, and the Voice repeated itself, "Enough!" I looked up from my arm, at myself in the mirror, and there was a clearer look in my eyes. Through the tears and through the pain, there was a light coming from my eyes, and I had a newfound awareness of what I was doing to myself. I looked back down at my arms, covered with rivers of blood flowing down to the floor. "I have already bled for you. Give me your pain. It is finished." I pulled the rig out of my arm and emptied its contents into the toilet. I took all the drugs I had in a bag on the counter and dumped them in with it. Courage and belief were overflowing that this was the last time I would do this, not an unfamiliar feeling from all the other times I have dumped drugs down the toilet. I took all the paraphernalia I had and put it into a box before taking it out to a dumpster. I then drove to a meeting and began the process I knew to do over again. Go to meetings, tell them you are suffering, and try not to use . . .

Journal Entry:

My God, my Father, look at me. Look at me as if You have never seen me, as if You do not know everything about me, from cell to cell, and as a judging human being. I ask of You to research me back up from each cell in my body, and attach them back together with the glue of the Holy Spirit. Search my mind for my knowledge, and let me know nothing You do not tell me. Search my heart for my gifts You have given me, and take them from me for You alone to use. Search my will to better know me, and erase it from my options. I want to witness Your will for my life worse than every currency of this world, worse than sin, and sleep. I Want You, God Almighty, to choose me.

PLEASE HELP ME!

IT WAS NOVEMBER 7, 2017, and by this point, I had been so beaten down in my life by the grips of addiction that I wanted to die; I was just unable to muster up what was needed to kill myself. I found myself in Veronica's car, weeping, in front of her place. I had tried everything and anything within myself to quit using drugs. The darkness, loneliness, humiliation, and despair had reached a tipping point my soul could no longer take.

> **Journal Entry:**
>
> *I guess it's the fear of telling you "I can't do it." Everyone close that doesn't suffer this feels I am needing to empower myself more. Some kind of thing I can do with my mind. I have officially tried everything within my power. I can't do this, and I don't know what exactly is going to happen . . .*

The Bible study I had been going to for the past five months every Tuesday was going to start in five minutes. I decided within my heart that I wasn't going. I decided that I was no longer going to try all these different ways to get out of this hell of a life I had created. I decided I was going to die on the streets alone and a drug addict.

When I came to this realization within my heart, I cried aloud in that car, "God! I quit! I'm done trying! Just take me now! I'm SO SICK OF THIS!" I wept some more.

As I sat there, alone in that car, conceding to my innermost self that I was going to die in this hopeless, lonely wreck of an existence, my Father in Heaven whispered into my heart, 'It's time. Go.'

I looked up through the ceiling of the car, and then back down into my hands, with a whimpering voice, "No, God. I'm so sick of this. I quit. Please just take me. There is nothing I can do. Please just take me."

'It's Time. Go.'

After I heard that voice a second time so clearly within my heart, the Spirit within me began to energize my body, and I could feel it fill me up with a confidence I hadn't yet felt in my life. I wiped away the tears and drove the little-over-a-mile drive to the coffeehouse where my men's Bible study met every Tuesday.

I remember when I pulled up, I had this mission. I didn't care what anyone thought. I had a LOT of drugs fighting their way out of my system, but that did not matter for the experience I had just had with God. I walked straight through the front doors of that coffee shop, with my chest leading me. I took a left to the conference room sliding doors, and swung them open twelve minutes late, interrupting the opening prayer, throwing my hands up in the air and yelling, "Guys, HELP ME! Please help me! I used again and I can't stop!!" I remember when I did this, I had the very distinct realization that I was not throwing my hands up to a fellowship. I was not surrendering to a Bible study to help me quit using. I came into that place to surrender to God. I had been beaten down to a point where I did not want my life anymore.

Here I was, a cracked-out mess, forty pounds underweight with bulging-out eyes, screaming in a Bible study for help. All the guys were giving me horrified looks from the circle of couches and seats.

Brendan got up and came over to me to calm me down. "Just chill. Let's get through Bible study." He always had this way of making every situation have a goofy undertone of 'Dude, it's cool. It's all good.'

I sat for the rest of the study and did my best to be quiet during it; I wasn't very good at that. I do not remember what the study was about, or where we were reading from, but I vividly remember what happened afterwards. Carmen, a man in the group with some spiritual gifts, came up to me and said he had gotten a word from the Lord about what to pray for over me. He, Brendan, and George stayed in that room after everyone had gone, and began to be witnesses to the Power of God.

I sat on the ottoman in the center of the room as Carmen stood in front of me, and George and Brendan to the side. I felt fear. I felt confused. I felt like I wasn't all there. Then Carmen looked me in the eyes, put his hand on my shoulder, and began to speak to evil spirits that were dwelling within me. He was pointing with one finger in my face and kept another hand on my shoulder, commanding things, in the name of Jesus, to leave me. I was aware the whole time, but I was in a different realm. I was feeling as things were leaving strangleholds on my heart. Whether he was praying away spirits of addiction, spirits of shame, or spirits of guilt and inadequacy, he was speaking directly to things I was feeling in the moment, and the feelings would leave me instantly.

This changed as soon as he called out the Spirit of the Occult. I remember feeling this thing come out of nowhere and overtake my body. I was looking him in the eyes until he called this out, and I looked down at my knees and said something funny that made those three laugh and Carmen look at the other two. As he was turning back to look at me, my face came up from the down position with a scowl of anger. I could feel my face doing this look, but I wasn't doing it. When Carmen made eye contact, I could see his face change to fear of me. I snapped out of it, and looked over to George and said, "George, get in here!"

George replied, "He's all right. He's got it," as Carmen turned me back to him with a firm grip on my shoulder. He continued to pray over me, and pray things out of me, for the next few minutes. I haven't used a drug or taken a sip of alcohol since.

Journal Entry:

If You are for me, who, then, could be against me? What could happen to me here that I would not be okay from, or after? What can man do to me that You have not already saved me from? I have no fear, for You are with me. You make known Your power around me every day in miraculous ways, and have used my lowest points to show me the most incredible grace and understanding. I do not wish lows in my life, because it does not serve You or others, but only me. But I trust You, Lord, and am ready for anything for Thou art with me. I only hear truth, because I requested it of You, but am aware of the attacks because I asked You for discernment. I only speak truth for You, because I listen for You in everything and everyone around me, and I am aware when Your Holy Spirit is causing me to speak. I say thanks to You, Father, in everything in every time past into eternity, and Praise the Highest and Holy Name of Your Son You gave me to save me from myself, Jesus Christ of Nazareth. Amen.

HIS FACE

FIVE DAYS AFTER THE EXPERIENCE at the Bible study, I went to IHOP with Brendan. He supported me through this whole process, and walked with me as I tried to get clean and connect with God. For those five days, I had not been delivered from obsession to use, and was what we addicts call 'white knuckling' through my days. I was pushing with everything in me not to use. We were having a good conversation, and I was confident in my discussion with him that I was done using. He, and everyone else in my life, had heard this multiple times before, but he continued being patient with me through the entire process.

We had finished eating our breakfast and were just talking with each other when I felt my phone vibrate with a text message in my front pocket. I pulled it out and opened the cheap little prepaid flip phone to find a text message from my dope dealer that read, "Hey, I just got some new stuff. It is FIRE. I'll give you a free twenty to try out."

At that moment, I felt the Spirit enter my body, just like my junior year of high school. It went from the top of my head throughout every crevasse of my body. I felt my toes tingle with Presence, my fingertips tingle with Presence, and then an extreme heightened sense of awareness as I lost all peripheral vision and was given tunnel vision at my phone screen. I then witnessed, under no control of my own, as my thumbs began texting my dealer back in a language straight from the King James version of the Bible. "Ye shall not text me again!" the text began, before the rest flowed out without me knowing what was going on.

My thumbs were moving without my mind telling them to. After the body of the text was finished, clearly letting him know I was crazy and not wanting any contact with him anymore, the last sentence that was written was, "And fear the pain you cause your son because your son has been blessed with the Holy Spirit." Right then, I felt the Spirit leave, from the tips of my toes, all the way through my body and out my head. I became aware of where I was again, looking at my phone in astonishment.

After coming to realize what was going on, and that I hadn't been the one who wrote that, I turned the screen to Brendan and said, "Dude, that was not me. I didn't write that!"

He read it, unaware of the experience with the Spirit I had just had, and probably thinking I was still a little crazy. He nodded and smirked with the patient reassurance he has as I began to tell him, "Bro, that was not me. I felt . . ." I pressed send on the phone, closed it, and began placing it in my pocket, looking down at my pants where I was putting it as I continued, " . . . the Spirit." As I looked back up from my pocket, Jesus Christ was sitting across from me. His Face was glowing in brilliance in front of Brendan. He blocked me from everything else in the world in that moment to see just Him. Everything around me became a blur, and an overwhelming sense of Peace that surpassed all my understanding flooded into my heart.

I immediately knew who He was and what was going on. I shut my mouth mid-sentence and fell with my face to the table, raising my right hand to the sky saying, "Thank You, God. Thank You,

God. Thank You, God!" And when I looked back up, He was gone. A sense of pure Joy flowed into me that I had never experienced before in my life. All the things I was experiencing throughout my life came to a head, and I then knew the Truth, no matter what anyone else thought or said. From all the experiences I'd had of the demonic, to the experience of the Spirit saving me from the shooting in high school, to the alley in Las Vegas, to the highway in Texas, and all the stories I couldn't fit in this book—it all came to that point, giving me the understanding of Who it had been the whole time. Jesus.

People sometimes ask me, "What did He look like?" It is impossible for me to describe the Magnificence of what I saw in His Face. There is no human way to describe what the Spirit of the Living God looks like when He reveals Himself to you. He had no race, there was no white European Jesus in front of me. He had a beard that was dark and wavy, and a smile that spoke more than any words could explain. His hair was long and wavy, and went down as long as His beard. He glowed. His Face was one size, but His presence was everywhere in that moment. It was like His Face took up the entire restaurant. There was nothing else around me. I now knew exactly who I was talking to in my prayers, and a newfound power and responsibility flowed into my life.

Now What?

OKAY, I HAD JESUS. NOW what? I was still white-
knuckling through my days and was having a very hard
time with life without drugs. I was regularly breaking down with
emotion and crying out of the blue. I remember ducking behind
a dumpster in the first ten days and falling to my knees, balling
my eyes out, asking for Jesus to help me through this. Although
I was unaware of any change to my feelings in that moment, He
was teaching me that feelings do not dictate the way I act.

In one of the recovery communities I went to, they taught to
pick up a service position and go to the meeting every night, and
don't drink or use in between meetings. I was never able to do
this. Even when I went to the meetings every day, I would have
to use in between. There were also twelve steps involved with
this group, and, for whatever reason, their conscious was to have
newly clean/sober people do one step per month. So, the
sponsor I had followed suit and was not taking me through the
steps with any urgency. I was emotionally and thoughtfully
falling apart, even though I now knew, without a doubt, who
God was.

I had moved into a sober living house, and was in a room with
five other men who were either coming out of prison, or were
newly clean/sober. One of the things I did at night to drown out
the sound of snoring and to continue seeking God was to listen
to tapes of speakers talking about recovery. On the eleventh day

of sobriety, while coming unglued and losing hope of being able to sustain this, a speaker-tape came over my phone that gave me a message that saved my life. This speaker began speaking directly to me through this phone and was saying things like, "Do the steps quickly! Do them as if your life depends on it! Because it probably does. Everything in this fellowship could be solved through good sponsorship."

As he continued, my heart began to listen from my ears, and I was not about to fall asleep. He talked about growing in life, and working on things outside of just trying to get clean/sober. I was infatuated with this message, and the Spirit was working in me so strongly, telling me that he was speaking to me, that when the tape was done, I quietly snuck out of my room to the kitchen table and began Googling the speaker. I found him, and after a few more clicks and tricks, I found a phone number for him. I called this number at 11:38 at night and got an answering machine. I leaned in over that kitchen table with a self-preserving intensity and began my message, "Chris, my name is Adam Gunton. I am a newcomer. I have eleven days, and I am coming unglued. I was just listening to your tape, and I am pretty sure you were talking directly to me. I need help. My number is . . ." And then I went back to bed for the night.

The next day, I was in line at the treatment center when I got a call on my cell phone from an area code I recognized from the night before. I walked out of the treatment center doors, opened my flip phone with a rush of enthusiasm, and yelled, "CHRIS? Is it you?"

"Yeah, buddy!" And thus started a friendship and mentorship that began my life-saving journey through the twelve steps. That day, I fired my sponsor after he would not let me go through the steps at my pace. The day after that, I went to coffee with a friend, Aaron, who had been there for me in some of the darkest times of my addiction. He came and met me at crack shacks I was staying at when I was on the brink of suicide. He just came in and sat with me. He would just come and listen, and that was the exact love I needed through those times. He ended up sponsoring me through the steps. He picked me up from the sober house every morning and took me to the movie theater he managed. We would sit in the basement, drinking coffee and doing the work together as if the world upstairs didn't exist.

On day twenty-five, I admitted to God, to myself, and to Aaron the exact nature of all my wrongs in life. This was something I had never done before, and up to this point had no idea what it even meant. The following day, Aaron came and picked me up like he had been doing every morning. I was looking out the window of his 1983 mailman Jeep at the sunrise cascading over the Montana plains when, suddenly, I had a spiritual awakening. I realized, for the first time since I was twelve years old, that I had no desire to drink or use any kind of drugs. The awakening was indescribable to someone who has not experienced it. It was like an entire displacement and rearrangement of thought patterns had happened overnight, stopping my thoughts from concluding to substance as solution. The unattainable dream was now my reality. I looked over at Aaron with wide eyes and a changed life, and said, "Aaron, thank you. I don't want to drink or use. I love you! Thank you so much!"

On day twenty-nine, knowing I was going to get thirty days the next day for the first time in my life, I asked my Bible study group to pray for me to not smoke cigarettes anymore. My morning journal from December 5th, 2017, reads:

> *Dear God,*
>
> *Thank You for my faith and everything going on in my life. I ask to get through today without a cigarette so I can prove to myself and others that I never have to drink, use, or smoke a cigarette again. Thank You for my 30 days sober so far, and for showing me I never have to drink or use again.*

I have not had a drag of a cigarette since. Every morning, I would pray in the shower and ask God to make miracles happen in my life and recovery so I can prove His Power to the people around me. I would pray for Him to restore my sanity, and for evil to be cast out of my life. I prayed that my mind would be restored, and my overall health would miraculously get better. On December 13th, eight days after quitting a pack-a-day smoking habit, I ran a mile in seven minutes and eighteen seconds. The God we serve is a miracle worker.

My mom and stepdad came up to Montana to visit, and were able to meet everyone who was in my corner during this process. It was an amazing feeling to see family after such a long time on hiatus. It was even better connecting with them with the Good News: I met Jesus! I established a strong connection with God in Montana, and soon after my sixty-day clean/sober date, I moved back home to Colorado and in with my sister. Now was the time to begin a life on track.

Journal Entry:

Dear God,

Thank You for my life. I am so blessed by You, and I want to be Your tool alone and no longer run my own life. If it is Your will, please help me to do what I must to stay clean and sober. I miss You. I have felt this shame, embarrassment, and fear for far too long. I know nothing of Your true power or plan for me, and I ask that You show me the way each day. I want to be a pen to Your story, but I am nothing without You. Please help me to stay clean so I may better understand and carry out Your plan for me. Please help me to be a better person. Please continue to show me Your communication that I feel in my heart to do the next right thing. I am so grateful for all the gifts You have given me, and I ask of You to show me the way to use them. Please help my family and loved ones to worry less each day until we can turn that worry into faith. I now know that this will not happen overnight, and I no longer have expectations of You to do this for me. Give me the strength to conquer my battles so they may be testimony to inspire others to conquer their own. I pray for my selfish ways to leave me, but to selfishly honor You. I pray for people to continually come into my path that will help me better serve You. I pray for the strength to begin a new life without the chains of drugs and alcohol. I pray for Your will to be recognized and understood throughout my days. I pray my failures no longer include substances that take me from You; that means all mind-altering substances. I pray for the people trying to help me to be given the words from You to me that I may better understand. I pray for forgiveness and to be a warrior for You through Christ. Amen.

Let God Use You

I WAS SITTING IN THE Mercury Café with a group of friends, preparing for the open mic. One of my new friends I had met on Facebook was sitting across from me, talking about a guy she had invited. There was a little bit of a love triangle with the other guy that was sitting on my left and the guy she invited, but I didn't think much of it. I was looking fresh, as always for the Mercury. I had my nice tight and suave jeans I got from Goodwill fitted on my legs. These were topped by my gold chain printed sweater and black blazer, with my little gold angel pendant on the left collar. We were in the middle of a conversation when a friend from a different lifetime ago walked in, immediately recognized me, and sat at our table. He was the guy my new friend was talking about meeting!

He said hi to her before turning his attention to me. It had been years since we had talked, but we had become fairly close in our raver group of friends about ten years earlier. He was telling his story about getting in trouble with the law and currently being on parole from prison when I looked down around his neck and noticed he was wearing the same pendant on a necklace as I had on my collar. I pointed at it, pointed at mine, and said, "Bro, that's a bit of a trip. Where did you get that?"

"My grandma gave it to me right before she passed. It's like my guardian angel."

When things like this start lining up, I have come to realize it is not synchronicity, as some people call it, but it is God letting me know I am in the right place. In the moment of things lining up, I don't always realize something crazy is getting ready to happen. Hindsight is 20/20, and when I look back, I can see how God is working. He loves to show off sometimes.

I only had a brief time to talk with him before it was my turn to get up on the stage and do my poem. I was doing the same poem from the day at the recovery event in the park. Whenever I get up and speak my truth to people, I get into what is called a flow-state. I am passionate and I believe that I am doing what I am supposed to be doing with my life. Whether there are two hundred people, or I am sharing it with one person, I feel like I am doing what I am supposed to be doing. This particular night, I could feel the energy coming from my heart as I shared this poem from the depths of my soul to a room full of strangers. I could feel my mind shut off and my spirit take over as my eyes watered and my face flushed with heat. I ended the poem in a different way than I ever had before with "We do recover . . ." and walked off the stage to an eruption of applause. I knew I had made an impact.

I walked over to my table of friends, who were all clapping and smiling at me, and looked up to notice a few strangers walking towards me. I always enjoy people coming up to me after I give my heart, and hearing what they have to say. It is always uplifting to know that an impact is being made, somehow, through me. The first girl that came up to me was beautiful. She had long, black hair and fair skin, with beautiful brown eyes from another world. "As you shared, I heard my brother's voice coming from your lips," she began. "He passed away a little over a year ago from a heroin overdose. He was never able to live up to his potential, and we miss him so much." One of her eyes started to water as she continued, "I heard him and felt like I saw him speaking through you. Thank you for sharing this tonight. It meant a lot to me."

Never hold back from telling someone
what they mean to you; You never know if
you'll get another opportunity . . .

I gave her a deep hug, and saw over her shoulder that there was another man waiting to speak with me. He was in his late fifties or early sixties with grey, stubbly hair on his face. He had his hands clasped and rubbing together while looking down at them to hide his eyes with the bill of his baseball cap. He took a step towards me, and raised his gaze from his hands to my eyes. In a low, pained tone, he asked, "Do you know Tabor?" My eyes widened slightly as my memory of a friend from a few years earlier popped into my mind. He was the first man I had asked to sponsor me in 2013. I had gone to his house a few times, but never got around to doing any work with him because I was caught up in a company I was trying to build. Tabor died of an overdose a couple years later.

"Yes," I replied. "He and I were close for a little while."

"Yeah, I knew it. I could smell him on you." His eyes began to water. "He was my son." He opened from his hidden posture and embraced me for a hug.

"I'm so sorry for your loss. He was a great guy." I hugged him tight, as if I had Tabor with me, hugging his dad. When I let go fifteen or twenty seconds later, he took a step back and had a grin on his face. He had gone from a sad father thinking about the son he had lost, to a comforted man who felt something he needed in that moment. Impact. He thanked me as he stepped away with a smile, and I sat back down at the table with my friends.

All these "synchronicities" lining up caused me to be totally present in the moment with an awe of the night I was having. I sat there at the table and really began taking in this experience while consciously thanking God. I was in my own world as I smiled and nodded at the friends at my table telling me how great of a job I did. I had just a few months away from drugs, alcohol, and cigarettes, so when my friends all got up to go outside and smoke, I stayed back at the table, sitting alone. This is when the night began to get crazy.

As I sat there taking in the environment and the next person's reading at the open mic, my spirit inside of me began to feel like it was trying to crawl out of my skin. It was very uncomfortable. It was as if something inside of me was growing at an uncontrollable rate and was unable to escape through the tent of skin trapping it. Then it began screaming at me in my head, 'We've got to get out of here! We are done here! Get out!'

I tried to shift a few times in my chair and look around for someone in the place that could help me overcome this feeling. I didn't see anyone. I couldn't stand it anymore, and stood up to step out and look for my friends. I noticed one of the servers I had had a few conversations with standing behind the curtain, preparing waters. I took the few steps over to her and leaned against the counter. It was as if my mind shut off! All I could get out was, "I just, um, thank you for being here."

She smiled up at me and said, "You're welcome."

'GET OUT!' my mind yelled at me, as my heart raced and my skin crawled.

"Welp, see ya later." I turned and walked away from her with an awwwwwwkward thought process rolling around in my head.

I needed to find my friends. Yeah, that was going to help. I went outside the front door, and a few steps to my left were the friends I was with. I walked up to them while they were in the middle of a conversation and smiled, with my awkward thoughts rolling around towards them, 'You realize I am going crazy right now and need some help calming down, right? You guys are my last option to make this go away. Will you talk to me and hug me or something and make me feel better?' Which came out as, "Sup."

They replied, "Sup."

'GET OUT!!!' my mind yelled at me.

"Welp, I gotta go, guys. See ya later." With an awkward smile and nothing else, I turned around and walked away from them towards California Street North on my way to Park Avenue, to go across where my car was. My mind began calming down as I headed that direction, and the spirit inside of me was now only pulling at my chest as if we were in the right direction. I still had just my little flip phone, and I pulled it out and began texting my spiritual advisor. "Dude," I typed, "There is absolutely no way this is real life. The things going on around me, the people I am coming in contact with . . . God is all over, dude. It is almost freaking me out! Thank you for being on the other end for me. I feel like you might understand." I pushed send, and I began to close the phone. I was five or six steps away from Park Avenue when I heard a man's voice come from the other side of the street:

"HEY! CAN YOU CALL 9-1-1!?"

I looked across the street to see a man on one knee, panicking next to a girl lying on her stomach with what looked like a bike on her back. At this moment, the spirit inside me had completely calmed down, along with all the things screaming at me in my head. I didn't even have to pull my phone out of my pocket—it was already in my hand, ready to go. I dialed 9-1-1 and felt like I was in a trance state of spirit-driven and protected action.

I walked across Park Avenue between two cross walks with cars coming at me in both directions when everything zoomed into a focus mode and slow motion. I stepped past one lane and a car would drive through it right after me. Then I stepped through another lane, and before I finished that one, a car would drive through the last one—one even drove past me in the lane in front of me with such precision timing that there had to be something much, much higher causing this to happen. I wasn't aware of all this until after the fact, because I was being driven by the Spirit inside me, and my mind had shut off to the world. I do not recommend walking into traffic while on your cellphone; however, if God is driving your body, you may not have an option.

As I stepped up the curb on the other side and saw a puddle of blood surrounding this woman's head, 9-1-1 answered. "9-1-1 Emergency, what is the location of your emergency?"

"Park Avenue, between California and Welton, on the north side of the street . . ." I knelt next to the man who had a panicked look, feel, and breath about him. I tilted the phone from my lips and put my hand on his shoulder, "It's going to be okay. They will be right here. What happened?"

The horrified look in his eyes as he was looking at her turned into a calmer, explanatory demeanor when his focus shifted to my eyes. "We were both riding on the sidewalk towards each other, and she looked up and saw me too late and swerved right into this pole. She's unconscious."

I relayed the information to 9-1-1, and before I could finish, the woman took one deep breath, with a painful moan, and began lifting her head out of the pool of blood. "She is waking up. Please hurry." She began to whimper, not knowing what was going on, and had her legs tangled up in her own bike, unable to get a good grip on her situation.

"Hey," I turned to the man, "Gently untangle her legs and pull her bike off to the side."

I put my hand underneath her bloodied head and calmly whispered, "You were in a bicycle accident. The ambulance is on the way. You are going to be okay." She began to cry, and as soon as her legs were untangled, I turned her on her side and rested her head in my lap. She went from a crying, bloody, and confused mess to a calm and inquisitive girl in my lap, looking up into my eyes. Her right eye was swollen shut and split open, needing stitches. Her other eye was staring into my eyes, as if she recognized me but couldn't figure out where from. I smiled. "You are going to be okay. Don't move anymore and just relax with me, okay?" She gently nodded once and continued to stare into my eyes.

At this time, the man involved in the accident had calmed down quite a bit. He said, "Man, thank you so much. I don't have my phone on me. I don't know what I would have done."

I just kept smiling at her, beginning to hear the sirens of emergency coming down Park Avenue.

She was asking, "What happened? What happened?" and repeated this, but never looked away from my eyes. In the moment, I felt a certain kind of peace I hadn't experienced before. It was as if, with all the chaos of life and circumstance in that moment, I had transcended into a state of oneness with the present moment. Nothing mattered. Nothing was scary. I wasn't worried about her, or me, or finances, or my career, or my contribution to life—just completely focused in the present moment. I wished that feeling would last forever, but the ambulance arrived and quickly needed me out of the way to brace her neck.

As soon as she was taken out of my lap and my gaze, she began to cry and panic. The police that arrived, as well as the paramedics, asked me about what I saw happen. "Nothing," I began. "Only walked over at the exact time after the accident to call you guys. I didn't see anything." They loaded her up onto a stretcher, and she was yelling, "No! No! I can't go! I have to go home!"

The paramedics were trying to calm her down while I was giving an account to the police, and I said, "Hold on a moment." I took the few steps over to the back of the ambulance and came to the bottom of her stretcher. I put my hand on her knee, looking her in the eyes. "Hey, everything is going to be fine. They are here to take care of you. God bless you." And I smiled, with my eyes looking directly into her one good eye.

She sat up just a little bit as the paramedics were pushing her back into the ambulance and said, "Wait! I know you!" before laying her head back in a completely calm state and looking directly up into the sky with a look of comfort.

I rarely know how God is using me in the moments that He is using me. I couldn't tell you what was going on in her head as she laid back into that ambulance and was taken to the hospital. I can tell you that the Spirit had that entire night planned in a way that I could never have imagined before leaving to go to the Mercury Café that night. One of my favorite verses in the New International Version of the Bible reads, "No eye has seen, no ear has heard, no mind has conceived the things God has prepared for those that love Him." I love being able to witness the Power of God in my life. I just need to figure out more and more ways for me to get out of His way in my life. Less of me, more of You.

Dear God,

As I move into this transition, I ask for You, Father God, to open the doors to my awareness of You. Let me know which doors You would have me walk through and shut the doors that are drifting me from Your will. I love You and am so grateful to You! I don't deserve this. You deserve me. You own me. I am Yours. Take me and deliver me from my flesh and desires, and use me however You will, O God, so I may be humbled more and more each day to Your plan.

EMMANUEL

I WAS NEARLY SIX MONTHS clean and sober, living at my sister's house back home in Denver, and enjoying the spiritual freedom that comes along with new sobriety. I was still seeking God in the morning, reading my Bible daily, and praying earnestly with thanksgiving. I was so elated to be alive that every day was a new blessing and a new joy to go out into the world. At that time, I was not working. My sister Amanda was happy to have me back in her and the family's life, and wanted to have me at the house to watch over my nephew, Elway—the most awesome little puppy in the whole wide world (this was *such* a hard job to do).

One late morning, as I was rolling on the floor with him in my room, my phone alarm went off with a reminder: Go to Civic Center Park for a speak-out against addiction.

A memory flashed of a few weeks earlier, when a girl in a fellowship told me about an event that was going to be held today, and me putting it in my calendar without a second thought. Then I thought, 'Hey, what the heck! Let's go see what this is about, God!' I ran upstairs, smiling puppy right on my heels, to shower up and get dressed.

Being the walking billboard of Jesus I am, I custom-made a hat with my favorite Bible verse embroidered on the front— "John 317" —*For God did not send His Son into the world to condemn the world but to save the world through Him* (NIV). I always loved the way God followed up the most famous verse in John 3:16 with the truth about why He sent Him. All the preaching in the world about sinful nature leading to hell is not going to save someone like me. I have been to hell. I have experienced hell on earth and there was nothing about the reality of its existence that was going to get me to submit to and follow Christ. We need to be preaching the Love, Peace, Joy, Abundance, Relationship, Hope, and fruits of the spirit that come along with life with Jesus. Anyway, where was I? Oh, yeah . . .

I threw on my Fresh Life Church sweater my mom bought me on her trip to Montana, put my cross-shield necklace on over it I had worn every day since I was sober, and covered it all with the hat that announced who my Lord is. I said bye to my nephew and hopped into my '99 Dodge Neon with the dented-in blue driver side door and flood-damaged ceiling to drive the fifteen minutes to Civic Center Park, not really knowing exactly what I was going to be a part of.

On my way, I started having thoughts of holding a megaphone or something, and yelling out, "We must stop addiction now!" Like, what the heck is a speak out against addiction? So, the whole time I was driving there, I was praying intently to God to the effect of, "God! I don't know what You have in store for me today, or who You have here for me to meet, but come with me! Work in the hearts of the people at this event, and prepare them for a message from You! May every word that comes from my lips be a Word directly from You! Prepare me, O God, to do whatever You have me going here to do!" I use a bunch of exclamations because excitement is how prayer is with me and God, much of the time. I love to get excited about what is happening in my life, and I love to include Him in everything because He shows up in amazing ways I could never imagine, as you will soon see in this story.

I arrived at the park and began walking around to look for the event. I found a group of people and a few tents and tables set up near the capital and walked over to it, noticing news cameras all over. 'News cameras?' I thought. 'I wonder what I have to do to get on those!'

I began talking to people who looked like they were part of the staff to find out information about exactly what I had just walked into. After talking to a few people, I ended up speaking with the director of the event that put it all together. It was a press conference for a new initiative in Denver called Lift the Label. This campaign is to stop the harmful labels put on opioid-dependent addicts that are causing them to not seek help. You can see the campaign on the Department of Behavioral Health's website.

I spoke with her for a minute and told her about how I had just over six months clean and sober. I told her about a poem I wrote that ends with the quote, "I'm leaving that label here—you can keep it." Not knowing she had some professional speakers and other guests coming to speak at the set-up podium, I asked what I would have to do to do this poem for the crowd that was gathered. She informed me that it was a very structured event, and then added at the end, "I can't let you on the news with that on your hat."

I thought to myself, 'Okay. I can understand why they wouldn't want to promote Jesus on Satan's broadcasting network.' Just kidding . . . But really, I thought that.

Austin Eubanks was at the event and was one of the main speakers who told his story. Having been from the Columbine community, I really loved to see the power in his message. [If you want to hear a very triumphant victory over addiction, I implore you to search for his Ted Talk on YouTube. To show the reality of what we are facing as a community, Austin was one of the biggest inspirations I had met for addiction recovery. Since writing this section of the book, he lost his battle with addiction, and the planet lost him. May his life continue to bless people in his death.]

After Austin finished, I looked over to the right of the crowd and noticed Governor Hickenlooper had just arrived. The director of the event got on the microphone and offered for him to skip the next speaker and come do his. He humbly said, "No. I will go after her," and stood by, listening to the next woman share her story. I began to feel a calling to go say hello to him, but he was covered with people and bodyguards, so I stood in my back-of-the-crowd spot and continued to listen to this woman share.

After she had finished her story, Hickenlooper came up to the podium and gave his perspective on the growing opioid epidemic. Everyone knows how bad this problem is, and many are attempting different forms of change to help the addicts still suffering. I wonder how many will be touched by the message of this book.

When he had finished and the event was breaking up, I had an urge in my heart to go over to him and say hello. There were a lot of people there, and I had to work my way through a crowd of men in suits, women dressed to impress, and little pockets of people conversing. I learned how to do this effectively in my years going to large electronic dance music festivals and always having to work my way to the front. If I am alone, I can do this without being a jerk or upsetting anyone. When I made it over to a clearing that opened to where he was with his security, I felt a change in the energy in the entire place. It was as if something had taken its total focus and shifted it on me and what I was doing and began trying to stop me. I felt an anxiety within my heart, and started hearing things in my head yelling at me, "You are so stupid! Don't go talk to him! You are a waste of his time! Why would he want to talk to you?"

I felt a pressure in my chest while noticing he was being ushered away by his security. The voices in my head continued to tell me, "He has to go! Stop wasting your time, and his!" I have come to recognize these as the principalities spoken of in Ephesians 6's forms of attack. I pushed through this spiritual force trying to stop me and took my last two steps towards him. As soon as his eyes turned to me, the voices and pressure disappeared as if I had just begun freefalling from a sky-dive, realizing the conquered fear had just become a blissful feeling.

"Governor," I began, "thank you for coming and for your involvement in this movement. My name is Adam Gunton." I stuck my hand out and he shook it immediately, looking me in the eyes. "I just got my six months clean and sober, and I am out to do big things with this crisis. I know you are a busy man; may I take a quick photo with you?"

"Good job on six months. Yes, hurry up, though, I've got to go." I pulled out my phone, put it on selfie mode, and took the photo below with the Governor:

Now, you may be wondering why I am taking so much time to tell you this story just to show you a picture of me and the former Governor. Well, it isn't just a photo of me and Hickenlooper. I posted this picture up on Facebook, and later that night, after I had gotten a few likes and the normal stuff that happens on Facebook, I noticed something that absolutely amazed me. Remember how the director had told me I couldn't be on the news with the hat I was wearing? Check out the wall behind me, right above my shoulder furthest from Hickenlooper. Jesus photobombed me! I did not go onto Facebook and begin to blast how cool it was or anything like that, and have reserved this story to close friends and family until now. After all the things I have been through in my life while asleep to the fact that He was always there, it feels great when He does things like this in my life to confirm how awesome He is. We can connect with the Creator of the entire universe!

A New Life –
A New Freedom

I AM NEARLY TWO YEARS free from drugs and alcohol. I have a business with over thirty employees, a new car, and a beautiful place in the heart of Denver overlooking downtown with a spectacular view. I attend a wonderful church with an amazing community and meet with my pastor and other leaders regularly. I live within a short drive of my family and see them on a regular basis—I just became an uncle and was given the honor of being my nephew Colton's godfather. I am surrounded by some of the best people I have ever known, and things are looking great for my future.

But something deep down inside is aching for meaning. Aching for purpose. And is finding that none of these things going on are going to fulfill it.

I saw an ad on Facebook with Kris Vallotton for a Christian business conference and booked a trip to Redding, California, to go to the Heaven in Business Conference, hoping to be able to bring meaning to the business I am in. I had a few weeks to go until the conference and continued about my everyday life. About two weeks before the conference, I was overwhelmed with a feeling of emptiness as I sat comfortably on my couch watching a television series before bed that was not "Kingdom-minded". All of a sudden, I got the urge to shut off the TV and go to the edge of my bed and pray:

"Father! I am SO SICK of this! None of this means anything to me! When I am praying and reading the Bible, I feel like I am not doing enough. And when I take time away from You, I miss you! I am sick of not being who you created me to be! Show me what I must do to speak, Father. I want to help millions. I want to bring you to millions, Lord. Show me what I must do, I will do anything. I love You. In Jesus' name."

And the Lord said,

"You do not need to do anything for
My Love. Do not worry. I am with you."

This short and simple exchange before bed made me sleep like a baby . . .

The next morning, before I did anything else, I got down on my knees and repeated a simple prayer, "Father, I am sick of not being who You created me to be. Show me what I need to do to speak. I want to speak, Father. I want to help millions." Then I got up and went about my morning routine:

1. Up at 4 A.M.

2. Run for one mile and meditate by the river.

3. Take vitamins, make coffee, and shower.

4. Bible study/time with God.

5. Read 30 pages of another book.

6. Goal setting/clarity.

While I was reading my book, a thought came to me suddenly: 'Text Ethan again.' Ethan is a friend of a friend who I had been introduced to through text a few weeks prior to this. He speaks in middle schools, high schools, and colleges around the country about his incredible journey through alcoholism and drug addiction. I texted him, asking to set up a call with him, to which he replied right away that he was available then to talk. We spoke for over an hour and decided to work together on an idea I have about going into schools as recovered addicts, and a system that can be shared with the world to systematically end addiction. He told me he was open to doing the first few for free to get the project off the ground, and asked me to get the first gig.

That day, I wound up with an appointment with the head counselor of a high school here in Denver, to which I went and closed the gig to speak with the students. My first speaking engagement at a high school just happened to be scheduled for November 6, 2019, my two-year clean and sober anniversary. That is a little over a month from now, as I write this to you with urgency, because I believe that is the date for this book to be released, as well.

I continued taking care of all my business responsibilities over the next couple weeks while planning and talking with God about how I am going to go about bringing a message into schools that will help save lives. This whole time, I am beginning to feel the sense of emptiness and meaninglessness leave my presence.

---

*Being passionately driven by Jesus' Purpose
is the only cure I have found to emptiness.*

The time came to head to Redding for the business conference. Everything went smooth with packing, getting a ride to the airport, hotel, car, everything. It was a great travel experience. I connected with a lot of great people at the conference, and had an amazing time sitting front and center for the whole thing. One day, as I was walking back in from lunch break, I saw a man standing in the back of the room that I recognized from online ads for another conference, 100X Academy, Pedro Adao. We locked eyes as I was walking up to him and both smiled. "I recognize you," I said with a smirk. "When is your conference, again?"

"Yeah, I saw you earlier . . . It's next week, bro." I looked away from him, in doubtful thought. "You should come, bro. It's going to be awesome. I'll introduce you to everyone."

Something inside me whispered through the doubts and fears of responsibilities back home and I said, "All right. Where do I go to buy a ticket?"

He showed me the website, and I bought a ticket standing there with him, and told him I would see him there. I went to the back of the room and sat down to buy my airfare as the session began. I have found that once airfare or hotel are booked to something, your mind makes it real. Buying a ticket to an event is not enough to live into the future; I had to commit, knowing I would have some explaining and words to have back home with my business partners.

When I bought my tickets for the conference I was at, I had left a few days on the tail end for me to be able to go to church services at Bethel Church. After the conference, I was beginning to have a lot of very weird thoughts about relapse. As I was driving by certain strangers on the street, a fleeting thought would come into my mind, 'I bet they know where to get some dope,' or, 'I bet they have some dope and would have everything we needed to get high right now.' It was weird, because I was having this amazing experience at this church I have wanted to visit since getting clean and sober. I shared with a friend the thoughts I was having, and let her know how they pop up occasionally, and I don't know why. I went to two services at Bethel, I witnessed someone's leg grow out in front of my own eyes in the healing rooms, met the speaker who spoke at the Sunday night service, and was told I was on the Livestream video of the service. But I experienced no freedom, no spiritual deliverance, no healing, and continued to have thoughts about relapse. Then another series of thoughts creeped into my mind, 'This is dumb. All these people are faking it. These people are ridiculous.' A confusing series of thoughts that I was beginning to believe.

It was time to travel home, where I would stay for two nights and one day. I got home after a long day of traveling to find that both of my white boards and my hanging chess board had fallen off the walls while I was gone, breaking the chess board, breaking a white board, putting a hole in one of my walls, and chipping a baseboard. 'Weird,' I thought, as I walked around my condo. I began to sense a heaviness, but was unaware of the gravity of what I was getting ready to endure.

Something did not want
me to go to 100x Academy . . .

The night I slept in my own bed before my flight back out to California, I could not, for the life of me, escape thoughts that were haunting me late into the night. I was unable to sleep, and laid alone in my bed for hours, tossing and turning with thoughts like, 'I should use. This life isn't worth it. I don't want to do all this. I could take all the money I have right now out of the bank tomorrow and have a really good run to Mexico. I should go get enough dope to kill myself. I should text everyone and let them know I am going to relapse until I die, and it is none of their fault. This is not worth it. I should not go back to California. The money spent doesn't matter where I am going. It would be so much easier to just be dead. Oh my gosh, it would feel so good to put heroin and meth in my arm.'

These thoughts were so incredibly heavy on me as I tossed and turned that my mind began to play out the vision of going to the old spot where I can pick up any day, any time, and getting dope. It went through a whole process of emptying my bank accounts and taking the cash to go on a last hurrah spree and killing myself. It was very oddly comforting. I was believing the thoughts coming into my head, and wanted to go use and die. At around 11:30, after laying with these thoughts for over two hours, with enough energy to stay up all night in these thoughts, I rolled over and picked up my phone and began texting people in my text conversations, "I love you." I sent some people a little more, as I was doing my best to try to get out of this depression.

I was using a method I created to escape from anxiety in the moment that I dubbed "complimentexting." The point was to text people deep compliments about what I think about them and think deeply about how much I love the person and why I love them. During the process of thinking about and writing about the other person, I would lose all the selfish thoughts going on in my head, which is the core of being prey to misery and depression: selfishness. For some reason, though, I was unable to muster up any selfless energy to come up with any good compliments and was trying very hard just to go through my contacts and text conversations to tell people I love them.

Aaron, one of the ones to whom this book is dedicated, got right back to me and asked me if he could call me. He has been there for me through so much in my life and was the only one I went into my phone contacts to search out and text; everyone else was in the recent text conversations I had up in my phone. We talked for a little while, and I told him all the thoughts I was having.

Sometimes, the best thing to do for someone is to just be present with them, and that's exactly what Aaron has done since I met him. After we hung up, I was able to fall asleep.

The next day, my flight was at 6:30 p.m., so I was able to hang out with a couple friends and get lunch. We were sitting in downtown Denver at a Menya restaurant for over an hour-and-a-half, having great conversations and witnessing firefighters and police working on a situation of a man on the ledge of a building, threatening to jump. I don't know what happened with him.

As we walked out, a notification popped up on my phone saying that my flight was leaving at 3:30! It was 2:09, and the airport is forty minutes away! Puzzled, I investigated it and realized my 6:30 flight was my connecting flight from Las Vegas, and I had totally dropped the ball. My friends and I began running back to my place to try to get me to the airport, and I kept repeating to myself, "That was so stupid. How could I have done that? I have never done that. So stupid." It was, in fact, so stupid and out of the norm for me that I was confused as to how it happened.

We got to the airport too late for me to board my flight, and I had to buy another one-way flight to get out there. I had already conceded the possibility on the drive there, so I was ready when I got to the airport. Then, as I was buying my ticket, I ran into Vanessa, someone from my church and one of my small groups who had moved to New York. Just a little bit of Jesus, saying hello.

The first night of the conference, God began to download ideas into my head that were very revealing to my calling and my purpose. As I worshipped to Jesus Culture, alone in the crowd of people, He gave me the name of my business/ministry this book is the start of, and I bought the domain name on the spot.

Throughout the weekend, I chose to go "all-in" on everything. I was sick of my life and the way things were going. I didn't want to continue to have thoughts about how unfulfilled I am living my life and figured I might as well go faithfully into this or I will end up killing myself. So, if there was a program that was going to serve my purpose, I jumped in. If there was a conversation where vulnerability could be shared, I jumped in. I shared with people about the thoughts I was having. I shared with people about my past. I shared with people the visions I was having as they came. And I ended up being asked to share my testimony on camera on the last day lunch break.

Through all this external act I was playing,
I was dying on the inside with a heaviness on my
shoulders and continuing to hear the voice of suicide.

On the last session of the last day, the speaker was on stage going crazy with his preaching. He was speaking in tongues, speaking about healing, and people were yelling and screaming and throwing their hands in the air by the stage. I stood back at my seat, alone, thinking, 'This is really over the top. This guy is crazy. These people are crazy. This is uncomfortable. I don't want to play into this.' These thoughts were the same thoughts my mind was having at the healing rooms at Bethel a week before. Something didn't want me up there.

I stood in the middle of the room by my seat, stiff-kneed with straight arms, placing my hands on the chair in front of me, and a weirded-out look on my face. A man I had met the night before and shared my thoughts with came over and put his hands on me. He began to pray in tongues. My mind continued, 'This is dumb. What are these people doing? Is this ever going to end?' Then Will, the speaker, looked directly into my eyes for a split second before turning away and immediately saying, "And I know there are some of you out there that are dealing with thoughts of suicide. I want you to come up here."

George, the man praying for me, gently let go with the hand that would guide me to the stage, and I felt as though something drove me to the front of the stage. It felt like I was almost gliding. I went through the crowd of people to the front middle of the stage. He said, "Raise your hand if this is you, struggling with suicide." There were about fifteen people in a crowd to the left of me with both of their hands up. I gently raised one hand about halfway. "Again," he continued, "raise your hand if this is you. I need to see you!" I raised my hand as high as I could for just a second. "If there has ever been a time you needed to pray for family, it's now. Extend your hands towards them."

At that moment, I felt hands come on to both of my shoulders, and as the speaker began inaudibly praying, I heard another voice come right into my ear from behind. "You are a son of the Most High God. You are loved unconditionally by the Father."

As he continued to pray in my ear, the voice in my head got much louder with, 'This is stupid! What do you want me to do? These people are crazy! Get off me!'

And the voice from behind me continued, "You have not been given a spirit of fear, but a spirit of love, power, and a sound mind . . ."

The voice in my head got very loud. 'Get off me! Get off me!'

"Sound mind! Sound mind!" were the last words I heard as my stomach began to rumble from the inside, and I heard a growl coming from my own mouth! As the rumble moved from my stomach up to my chest, I went unconscious and woke up on the floor, on my back with Will, who was previously on the elevated stage, laying on top of me, hugging me and repeating, "Radical love! Radical love! Radical love! Your Father loves you so much!"

My eyes were trying to come back into focus, and they were watering—well, I was crying. I didn't know what was going on. I had a man's face right in front of mine, telling me how much he loved me, with a huge crowd of people looking down from all around me. "Soak the love in, brother. Stay there for a few minutes." As he got off me, other people began coming down onto the floor and touching me and telling me how much they love me. It was overwhelming at first, but got more and more comforting as people were talking to me. I began realizing an absence of something that I had not felt absent from in a long time. I felt like a voice had left my head that had been there for a very long time. I was still lying on the ground, but felt like I was floating in the sky with angels all around me.

Then a man knelt beside me and began speaking with me, smiling and encouraging me about what had just taken place. I was coming more into myself and was ready to get up off the floor, so he took my hand and helped raise me to my feet. "How do you feel?" he asked.

I had great big, wide eyes looking around the room because I was seeing colors brighter, I was seeing faces more beautifully, I felt lighter, and like my breath was going deeper into my lungs. "I see clearer. Everything is popping out at me. Everything is beautiful. I feel lighter. What is going on?"

He smiled, took hold of my hand firmly, and turned toward the stage, towing me behind him.

Someone from on the stage helped him up onto the stage, and then he helped me up onto the stage. I turned to see the crowd of seven hundred or more people in front of me and the cameras all around the room. It was surreal. I felt like I was looking at a dream I had had before. Will came over to me with the microphone and handed it to me, saying, "Tell everyone what just happened. Don't worry, I'm right here . . ." Comforting, yet I wasn't worried—this is what I was born to do.

As I told the story of what had just happened, everyone in the room was shouting and praising God. I was still in a state of disbelief, causing an awkward grin as I shared the testimony.

When I finished, I handed the mic back to Will, smiling from ear to ear at what was going on. He leaned into me and said, "Now, pray for those out there struggling with suicide," before handing me the mic and repeating, "Don't worry. I'm right here." It was like God speaking directly through him, and my thought of confidence was reassured as I closed my eyes and began to praise and thank God for all I have been through.

Everything in my journey that had led to this point in my life was coming out in praise and thanksgiving in front of thousands of people. At the end of praise, and as I started moving into prayer, my mind shut off and I could no longer think about the words I was saying as they were coming out. There was an Authority behind me that was not my own. I witnessed words coming from my mouth that were not coming from my mind, but were coming directly from my heart without any fear of what people were going to think. The Holy Spirit took over and spoke through me. I opened my eyes, with my hands in front of me, as I loved and thanked God again, and in that moment, I remembered this exact vision from a dream I had had years earlier. My hand out in front of me, with tattooed arms and hands, holding a microphone and speaking from a stage to a crowd I could not see.

When I got home from the conference, I was incredibly inspired to take massive directed action. I have been writing and writing and writing this book I have been wanting to release for years of my life. Part of the issue was my fear of whether people would believe me. Whether or not people would think I was crazy. This experience with the demonic realm defeated by the power of God in total sobriety, witnessed by many, solidified my belief in myself. I am no longer afraid to share my story. I pray my story will encourage someone else to release their own story. I pray this book will give hope to an addict suffering, and to their family members. I hope this book will help people understand the spiritual war going on for the souls of this planet. I hope this book will help.

One last thing, as I sat down to write this final chapter of this book, God revealed the date of my deliverance from the spirit of suicide: September 28, 2019. Exactly eleven years since that life altering experience with Chuck's suicide. I pray this testimony can cut someone else's struggle from eleven years down to stop right now. Seek help. Be open with what is going on within you. Know that those thoughts are not your own and there is freedom. I pray, in Jesus' name, that spirit leaves anyone reading these words and never come back. May the full grace and mercy of the Lord Jesus Christ bless you in every way. Welcome to a free and saved life. God bless you.

About the Author

Adam Vibe Gunton is an author, speaker, and entrepreneur who is driven by a mission to add purpose and meaning to as many lives as possible. With this book, he hopes to give essential hope to addicts still suffering that there is a life beyond addiction to drugs. He believes every addict is on their own journey to recovery and believes that every addict knows the steps they must take to bring themselves out of their addiction; it is up to them to do it.

Once an addict has abstained from drugs and alcohol, Adam is passionate about connecting them with purpose and meaning for their life. He hopes this book can be living proof to recovered addicts that it is not only possible, but necessary, for them to get their stories out to the public. He believes every addict's story of overcoming addiction is a vital asset to society.

You can connect with Adam Vibe Gunton through his Facebook page by sending him a message. He loves to hear from people that have read his book. If you would like to book Adam Vibe Gunton to speak at your school, treatment center, or event, you can email his admin at RecoveredOnPurpose@gmail.com.

If this book has touched you, and you know someone that fits in those two categories, please, get a copy of this book in their hands. You never know the power of a timely message to someone in need. Thank you so much for your continued support and I look forward to connecting with you.

Made in the USA
Middletown, DE
12 November 2021

52258868R00087